1.50

All you need is Christ

All you need is Christ

STUDIES IN GALATIANS

Steve Brady

with Sheila Jacobs

Keswick
ministries
bringing the Word alive

Authentic

LONDON ● COLORADO SPRINGS ● HYDERABAD

13 12 11 10 09 08 07   7 6 5 4 3 2 1

First published 2007 by Authentic Media
9 Holdom Avenue, Bletchley, Milton Keynes, Bucks, MK1 1QR, UK
1820 Jet Stream Drive, Colorado Springs, CO 80921, USA
OM Authentic Media, Medchal Road, Jeedimetla Village,
Secunderabad 500 055, A.P., India
www.authenticmedia.co.uk
Authentic Media is a division of IBS-STL U.K., limited by guarantee, with its
Registered Office at Kingstown Broadway, Carlisle, Cumbria CA3 0HA.
Registered in England & Wales No. 1216232. Registered charity 270162

British Library Cataloguing in Publication Data
A catalogue record for this book is available from the
British Library

ISBN-13: 978-1-85078-748-8
ISBN-10: 1-85078-748-4

Cover Design by fourninezero design.
Print Management by Adare Carwin
Printed and bound in Great Britain by J.H. Haynes & Co., Sparkford

This book is dedicated to the members of the churches I have served at Hyde Heath Bucks; Knighton, Leicester; East London Tabernacle and Lansdowne Baptist Bournemouth, and generations of staff and students, Moorlands College, Christchurch.

Contents

THE AIM OF THIS STUDY GUIDE

In this study guide, Steve Brady takes us through the book of Galatians, with its emphasis on the freedom we have in Christ and the all-sufficiency of his death on the cross for us. This book is designed to help you to get the most out of this wonderful letter of Paul.

The questions in each chapter help relate the principles explained in the commentary to your own lives and situations. You can use this guide either for your own devotional time with God or as a part of a group. Enjoy your study.

USING THIS BOOK FOR PERSONAL STUDY

Begin by praying and reading through the passage and commentary a number of times before looking at the questions.

You may find it helpful to note down your answers to the questions and any other thoughts you may have. Putting pen to paper will help you think through the issues and how they specifically apply to your own situation. It will also be encouraging to look back over all that God has been teaching you.

Talk about what you're learning with a friend. Pray together that you'll be able to apply all these new lessons to your life.

USING THIS BOOK IN A SMALL GROUP: FOR GROUP LEADERS

In preparation for the study, pray and read the passage of Scripture and commentary over a number of times. Use other resource material such as a Bible dictionary or atlas if it would be helpful. Before each session, look through the specific materials you need for that study – see the chapter breakdown below.

At the top of each chapter we have stated the aim – this is the heart of the passage and the truth you want your group to take away with them. With this in mind, decide which questions and activities you should spend most time on. Add questions that would be helpful to your group or particular church situation.

Before people come encourage them to read the passage and commentary that you will be studying each week.

Make sure you leave time at the end of the study for people to 'Reflect and Respond' so they are able to apply what they are learning to their own situation.

All you need is Christ

INTRODUCTION

Many people believe the chief purpose of the Christian faith today should be to provide an ethical framework for a confused and confusing world. In the UK, governments have regularly called on the Church to give a moral lead to the nation. In addition, there are millions of people, outwardly honest and sincere, who believe that some kind of faith in God (however defined), occasional attendance at a religious ceremony – you choose! – and some commitment to follow 'the golden rule', will mean that, on the whole, God will be pleased with them. Indeed, the Deity would be almost duty bound to reward them with an entrance ticket to heaven, if John Lennon's sentiments – *Imagine there's no heaven* – are incorrect.

Paul's letter to the Galatians comes as a terrific shock to most people. It is a very dangerous book. Firstly, it straightforwardly reminds the religious and the irreligious that everyone's greatest need is to be right with God – the doctrine of justification by faith. Secondly, it is a warning that religion can be bad for our spiritual health – it may rob us of the experience of God's grace that brings salvation. Thirdly, it challenges so much of the legalism and religiosity found in many local churches: 'Christ lives in me' trumpets Galatians. Yet so many believers seem to behave as if Jesus never rose from the dead. 'It is for freedom that Christ has set us free,' shouts this letter. So how come so many Christians live in spiritual bondage? Christians are 'All one in Christ Jesus', the Keswick Convention's motto, yet so many of our churches are divided by petty squabbles and holier-than-thou attitudes.

Galatians is a breath of fresh air blowing through the musty and dark cells of human imprisonment, perversity, despair and death. It proclaims that the Liberator has come to set us free; the Redeemer has arrived, right on time, to bring us home to God.

Welcome to this revolutionary letter, the 'Magna Carta' of the Christian faith. Here's the gospel of astonishing grace that justifies sinners and turns slaves into saints through 'the cross of our Lord Jesus Christ.' This letter, perhaps one of the first Paul ever wrote, written to a group of churches of whose location we are not totally sure, is dangerous – and revolutionary. Are you ready for a bumpy ride to spiritual freedom, from slavery to sonship? Step this way, fasten your seat belt for the ride of your life. I pray this magnificent part of Scripture will change and deepen your experience of Christ for ever.

CHAPTER 1

The New Age Gospel

GALATIANS 1:1-5

Aim: To examine the authenticity of Paul's gospel

FOCUS ON THE THEME:
If you open a tin labelled tomato soup, you don't expect to find fruit cocktail inside. If a product promises a certain result, you expect it to do exactly what it says on the tin. As we study Galatians, we will see that 'Paul's gospel' was the same as that of the other apostles: no nasty surprises, no hidden agendas, no complicated extras we didn't know about. We can trust in his teaching – unlike that of other philosophies and spiritualities, where opening a beautifully-presented tin promising so much can result in disappointment, emptiness . . . and danger. What products have you found have lived up to the advertisers' claims – and which ones haven't? Go quickly round the group and say how you feel when you discover some claims are spurious.

Reading: Galatians 1:1-5
Key verse: Galatians 1:1

There he was, saffron-robed, shaved head, bare feet, dancing and chanting in downtown Birmingham. A young student from the University, a Christian, had the opportunity to explain to him his need of Jesus Christ as Saviour and Lord. The barefooted devotee could neither stand nor understand what he was hearing and finally exploded, 'Man, you sure are weird!'

'New Age' is a slippery term, covering philosophies and spiritualities from Zen Buddhism through to Scientology, and is increasingly popular in the western world. Why the interest? The reasons are varied but for some, I suspect, it is the sheer dissatisfaction with materialism: after the second home, second car, second career, many discover, in the words of a song from Sting and the Police, 'There's a hole in my life.' Many people are aware of their impotence, insignificance and isolation and are looking for answers to the emptiness inside. The answer – a personally cooked spirituality from the à la carte New Age menu. Who would have thought that all these philosophies and spiritualities have already been trumped by the coming of Jesus and the birth of his Church?

The astounding news is that the 'New Age' is not about to dawn; it has. In essence, it is all found in Jesus 'who gave himself . . . to rescue us from the present evil age' (v4). Christianity is a rescue religion. It is all about God plunging into our sea of human lostness and, through the death and resurrection of Jesus, saving people decisively and for ever. The true New Age is already upon us, and it is found in the good news of Jesus, 'God the Rescuer.'

The problem with the Galatian churches, and many modern ones, was they were in danger of forgetting Jesus and dismissing 'Paul's gospel' as just that: his '(per)version' of the gospel. Such a 'gospel' needed to be challenged and supplemented, they said, especially (as we shall see) by marks in the body (circumcision) to show who really belonged to God. So why stay with Paul's gospel? Here he gives three solid reasons.

CHRISTIANITY RESTS ON A SAVING HISTORY

Here is the unique and decisive thing about Christianity. Religion may offer experiences; new religious movements may meet many of our felt needs. But Christianity stands or falls with its appeal to facts, that the events it records actually happened. In these opening verses, Paul reminds us of a number of them.

First, it is all to do with what God the Father has done through Jesus. I suspect that if you extracted Buddha from Buddhism or Confucius from Confucianism, their respective faiths could survive. But remove Jesus from the New Testament and from the pages of history, and you'd have to reinstate him, because he is the only way to make sense of the Bible or the world in which we live. You cannot have Christianity without Christ. He is a unique Person, 'the Lord Jesus Christ' (v3). For Paul, though Jesus was not less than a real human being, he was far more. Notice how Paul was 'sent not . . . by man, but by Jesus Christ' (v1) and how the 'grace and peace' that flow to us come not only from 'God our Father' but also from 'the Lord Jesus' (v3). He is more than a man. He comes from the divine side of reality. The fact is that 'God sent his Son' (Gal. 4:4). He is the *Lord Jesus Christ: Lord* because he's God, *Jesus* because he's Saviour and *Christ* because he's the promised Deliverer and King. This unique Person has given a unique gift. Jesus gave not only his time, talents and energies. It was far more: he gave 'himself.' Why? – 'for our sins' (v4).

No religion in the world takes sin more seriously than the Christian faith. Sin is the great barrier between a holy God and ourselves. It is behind all that is wrong with our world. And we are all part of the problem – 'all have sinned' (Rom. 3:23). But Jesus has dealt with it at the cross, dying in our place. Sometimes this picture has been caricatured: an angry God is appeased by a loving Jesus. This is not so: behind the giving of Jesus is the Father's will (v1) and the Father's love (see John 3:16: 'For God so loved the world that he gave. . .') Christ died in real space and time, one day on a cross outside Jerusalem, a fact of history.

So why bother with him today? Very simply, it is because Christianity's Founder is still alive (v1).

What proves the uniqueness of Jesus beyond doubt? It's the resurrection (Rom. 1:4). Do you want to be sure that his offering of himself on the cross is enough? In Old Testament times, the High Priest went into the Holy of Holies on the Day of Atonement and there he sprinkled the atoning blood of sacrifice (Lev. 16). How did the worshippers know that God had accepted the sacrifice? Because the High Priest emerged from that act alive. Christ went into death and God raised him from the dead – he's emerged alive!

The resurrection of Jesus has everything to do with the New Age. The Jews expected a new age to dawn when the Messiah came, delivering them 'from the present evil age' (v4) and raising the dead. But here at a specific point in history Christ has been raised from the dead. The result is that our clocks and calendars have been recalibrated. The resurrection of Jesus heralds the new 'Greenwich Mean Time' from which all of subsequent history must check what time it is. The New Age has dawned in Jesus. Through him, it has been inaugurated and will one day be consummated. The real problem with present day 'New Agers' is they don't know the right time. Without Jesus, we are still in the 'present evil age', whatever we believe. But in Jesus, I do not have a guru who is or will be dead and gone; I have a Saviour and Lord who is alive for ever (Rev. 1:18). Christianity rests on certain facts, facts of first and central importance: Christ died and rose from the dead for us (1 Cor. 15:3,4). But there's more.

● *Think about the uniqueness of Christ. Why is the Deity of Christ so crucial to both our understanding of his Person and his work?*

● *'Believing God is an angry God appeased by a loving Jesus shows an incorrect understanding of Scripture, the love of God, and the teachings of his Son.' Do you agree?*

CHRISTIANITY RELIES ON APOSTOLIC AUTHORITY

Dan Brown's *The Da Vinci Code*, a runaway best seller and blockbuster film, has a very simple thesis: the origins of orthodox Christianity are wrong. The truth is out there, somewhere else. But there's nothing new here. Something akin to that kind of notion was going on around 50AD in Galatia. Paul had it wrong. He could not be a bona fide apostle, for he was not one of the original Twelve. His credentials were 'dodgy', when compared to those authentic apostles in Jerusalem (2:9). But Paul insists that he was 'an apostle – sent not from men nor by man, but by Jesus Christ and God the Father' (v1). Indeed he received his gospel straight from Jesus (v12).

Like 'New Age', 'apostle' is a loaded and slippery term today. Basically, it means 'sent one.' For example, Jesus is called our apostle, as he was sent by God (Heb. 3:1). In a wider sense, Jesus sends every Christian to serve him in his world. The Latin equivalent of the word is 'missionary.' In addition, there are 'apostles of the churches' referred to in 2 Corinthians 8:23 ('representatives') and Philippians 2:25 ('messenger').

In Paul's world, however, 'apostle' also had a more technical meaning – somebody sent as the fully authoritative representative of another, like an ambassador. He delivered the word of the sender, perhaps a king, standing in as a full representative. There's certainly some of that meaning behind the usage here. But he intends even more. 'The Twelve' were that unique group of men whom Christ personally commissioned. Now that put Paul in a difficult position. Acts 1 laid down qualifications for Judas's replacement (Acts 1:21-22) – and Paul did not have them! So how could he be anything other than an inferior apostle, whose particular brand of Christianity could be safely ignored? The answer is found in what he has to say in, for instance, 1 Corinthians 9:1f and 15:8-11. There he claims to have seen the Risen Christ and have been commissioned by him. Such a theme continues through this chapter: check out verses 17 and 19 where apostle is being used in that narrower, primary sense of someone uniquely commissioned by Jesus to preach the gospel. Is this relevant today? It certainly is when we consider issues about succession, cessation or restoration.

Apostolic succession

This is a major doctrine in Roman Catholic and other churches' teaching. The belief is that there is an unbroken line back through various Popes to Peter, the first of them, and the leading apostle. But if the apostles were unique, in that they had personally seen the Risen Christ, then the real apostolic succession is found elsewhere, in the truth of the gospel recorded in the Bible.

Apostolic cessation

At the other extreme, this can also be called 'superannuation': that is, the apostles and the Bible have been retired, pensioned off. They have been replaced by a liberal theological elite who think Paul is wrong and venture to say so. Then, Christianity becomes something that it foundationally never was: the apostles got it wrong on various things, but we can make it right, or even make Christianity up as we go along.

Apostles' restoration

There are different versions of this, everything from the heretical to the orthodox. Undoubtedly, God has raised up remarkable people through the history of the Church who have, like the original apostles, founded churches and had a trans-local church ministry. The great Chinese Confucian scholar turned Christian leader, Pastor Hsi, well deserves the phrase 'apostolic', used by the brilliant twentieth-century preacher Dr Martyn Lloyd-Jones, to summarise Hsi's monumental labours for Christ in China. Thank God for every apostolic pioneer planting gospel churches. What, however, is precluded from the definition is the idea that there are Christian leaders, since the time of the original apostles, who are on the same level with Paul, Peter or John in terms of being bearers of revelation not found in Scripture. One of the very reasons the canon of Scripture came together, contra *The Da Vinci Code*, was to ensure that the Church remained true to the revelation she had received from the Risen Lord through his apostles and prophets of the first century. If 'new' revelation did not tie in with that, it was rejected. That's why 'Paul's gospel' was not Paul's – it was the Lord's, the same gospel his fellow apostles preached (2:7-9).

In a pragmatic age like ours, the foregoing to some people may seem too theoretical. Does the gospel work? Does this gospel of Paul/Jesus/the apostles change anything? It certainly does.

● *In Acts 5:38 we read of a leading Pharisee who said that if the apostles' purpose was from God, no one would be able to stop them. In what ways can we see that Paul's apostleship was the same as the rest of the apostles?*

CHRISTIANITY RELEASES FROM SPIRITUAL CAPTIVITY

What is the attraction of New Age movements and Doomsday cults? At their best, they offer the devotees a path to enlightenment, personal wholeness and liberty, either in this world or the next. Sometimes the claims are extravagant in the extreme. A limerick puts it this way

> A famous faith healer from Deal
> Said, 'Although I know pain is not real,
> When I sit on a pin,
> And it punctures my skin,
> I don't like what I fancy I feel.'

We are all aware that all is not well with planet Earth. Indeed, it is this 'present evil age' that is a world out of kilter with God and itself because of sin. An alternative translation would be the age of the present evil one, that is the devil himself, who is behind this present evil age, pulling the strings of wickedness, wreaking havoc in homes and hearts and lives, the prince of deceit and lord of darkness. Spiritual deception is nothing new. It is as old as the gospel, and if the gospel of Jesus is not believed, we can be sure people are believing something else that keeps them from Jesus. Could that explain why so many are fascinated by alternative spiritualities and philosophies? It is possible to exchange 'the truth of God for a lie' (Rom. 1:25). But the gospel is a rescue mission to save us through the Christ who died 'for our sins' (v4) and liberate us from evil and the evil one (Col. 2:14f). When a person yields to Jesus Christ as Saviour and Lord, there's a 'new creation' started in that person's life (2 Cor. 5:17). Old bondages are gone, sin is forgiven and new life is imparted to be lived to the glory of God.

How is this accomplished? God has raised Jesus from the dead. Everyone united to him by faith is simultaneously forgiven and receives a new life by the Spirit of God. Christians are the real 'New Agers' because, through the Risen Lord, a new world has begun. Sure, it's not here in its fullness yet. So we pray 'thy kingdom come.' But its coming is inevitable, it is 'the will of our God and Father' (v4).

● *Many people dabble in alternative spiritualities, without realising that their basic problem is one of sin and the need for a Saviour. How can you share this with them without alienating them?*

CONCLUSION

Why should anyone be a Christian? Because Christianity deals with objective facts – it really happened, Christ died and rose again. This is not just a philosophy or a way of looking at the world. How do we know? We have apostolic testimony, apostolic documents found in the pages of our Bibles. Does it matter? Of course it does. When we believe in Christ we are no longer in spiritual captivity but free, no longer blind but see.

How does it happen? By 'grace', God giving us what we don't deserve, and bestowing 'peace' (v3) with God, others and myself, as a result. Our response should be to give 'glory for ever and ever' (v5) to our God in Christ. Unlike New Age philosophies, the gospel places God, not me, at the centre, giving him the credit. When this letter was read to the original churches, their response would have been 'Amen!' Let's make it ours.

FURTHER STUDY
Read Acts 7:54 – 8:1a. Then read Saul's encounter with Jesus in Acts 9:1-19. Surely only a supernatural meeting with Jesus could change someone so radically. Do you agree?

REFLECTION AND RESPONSE

• Reflect on the fact that Christianity releases us from spiritual captivity. Jesus proved he had power over Satan by healing the sick, casting out demons and forgiving our sins. He is the One who can release us from the darkness of Satan's rule in our hearts, minds and lives. Consider how encountering Jesus changed Saul of Tarsus. How has Jesus changed you? What else needs to change?

• Praise God for his rescue mission. Trust him to complete the work in you that he has begun, as you grow in wisdom and understanding during this study.

• You might know someone caught up in an alternative spirituality. Pray for them that they will find Jesus as their Rescuer and that he might change their lives too.

SMALL GROUP DISCUSSION POINT

Discuss why the New Age gospel can be so attractive today to the 'me' generation who want to fill the spiritual gap in their lives. What do New Age beliefs offer that Jesus doesn't? Think about keeping a journal during the duration of this study, marking important points learned each week, so you will have a record of what you have learned.

CHAPTER 2

Perverted

GALATIANS 1:6-10

Aim: To challenge us to live to please 'the audience of one.'

FOCUS ON THE THEME:
Once, a man had to make a long trip with his son and his donkey. They set out with the man riding the donkey, but before long they met a fellow traveller who said, 'How selfish of you, riding whilst your poor little son has to walk.' So the man got off the donkey and let his son ride instead. Further on, another traveller stopped them. 'How selfish of you, young man, letting your poor old father walk whilst you ride!' So the son and his father decided – they'd *both* ride. But further along the road, yet another traveller told them, 'How selfish of you, both riding that poor little donkey!' In the end, the father and son reached their destination walking and exhausted, beside the donkey. The people laughed at them. 'Fancy walking all that way,' they jeered, 'when you've got a perfectly good donkey to ride!' You can't please everyone! Share any situations where you have felt you have tried to please more than one person but have ended up pleasing no-one – including yourself.

Reading: Galatians 1:6-10
Key verse: Galatians 1:10

In the UK today, we are rightly concerned about perversion – those moral perverts who exploit children and the vulnerable. It may be expressed by paedophilia or the trafficking of young men and women into prostitution and slavery by the lure of jobs, money and a better life in another part of the world. However heinous such moral perversion is, there is something worse. At the back of the moral landslide that we have witnessed in Great Britain over the last forty years is a spiritual collapse, a loss of faith in anything greater than what is immediately gratifying. In this section, Paul deals with an abandonment of the gospel of Christ that inevitably leads to spiritual perversion which, in turn, has profound moral and ethical implications.

THE GOSPEL CAN BE PERVERTED

'Some . . . are trying to pervert the gospel of Christ,' Paul asserts in verse 7. Normally in his letters, at this early point, Paul would compliment the recipient in some way (for example, see 1 Corinthians 1:4-9). So we might expect verse 6 to say something like, 'I thank God for your faith and I'm praying for you to press on.' But when he writes to the Galatian church, he immediately gets to the point, pulling no punches: 'I am astonished that you are so quickly deserting the one who called you by the grace of Christ and are turning to a different gospel.' He wants to stop these converts from deserting Christ. They were in danger of becoming 'spiritual perverts', corrupters of the gospel of Jesus Christ.

The gospel of Jesus has never lacked perverters – those who want to change it, edit it, add to it and so turn it into something different. Church history is full of examples, and so is the contemporary world – again, witness the amazing publishing success of *The Da Vinci Code*, and a whole industry of paraphernalia spun from it. What astonished the apostle was that the rot threatened to set in so quickly, so early on in their Christian lives.

Verse 7 reminds us that the gospel is the good news of *Christ*, the long-promised King of the Old Testament Scriptures, the one who would deliver his people from their enemies. The gospel centres on a unique Person, the Son of God, whom God raised from the dead (v1). So to abandon the gospel is to abandon Jesus, since he is the good news, the big story-line of the whole Bible.

This gospel not only reveals how great Christ is, but tells of the wondrous love that led him to give himself 'for our sins to rescue us' (v4). Later in the letter, Paul will apply this truth personally: 'I live by faith in the Son of God, who loved me and gave himself for me' (2:20). Why did Jesus do what he did? It is summarised in the great gospel word, 'grace', that calls us without any merit on our part, back home to God (v6). There on the cross Jesus cried 'Finished' – 'paid', if you prefer (Jn. 19:30). No matter how morally polluted and sunk in sin we are, there is hope in the Crucified One who paid the price of our forgiveness. As Paul will remind us in 2:16 (three times, if you look carefully), it is through faith in Christ, not our performance, that such forgiveness and welcome are received.

What was the major problem in these Galatian churches? We may recall that all the first Christians were Jewish. That meant obeying the law. But how can we tell if someone really is loving God with all their being (Deut. 6:5), since we cannot see the heart? By this time there were three major indicators: circumcision for every male, sabbath observance and following a *kosher* diet. Follow these rules and you were clearly part of the 'in-crowd.' Then a revolution took place in the Early Church: pagan Gentiles began to come to Christ (Acts 10, 11 and 15). Should Gentiles first become Jews in order to be Christians, and take on the obligations of all that law-keeping ('Unless you are circumcised . . . you cannot be saved', Acts 15:1)? The answer from some was 'Yes.' Such teachers were 'throwing . . . into confusion' (v7) these mainly Gentile converts. Can we see how disastrous that ultimately is? It means that the death of Christ is not therefore enough – 'Christ died for nothing', as Paul will later state (2:21). In addition, these false teachers were also undermining Paul's preaching, by suggesting that his version of the gospel was not the full gospel, an issue to which he will return in these opening chapters.

Paul's response is electrifying: 'But even if we or an angel from heaven should preach a gospel other than the one preached to you, let him be eternally condemned!' (v8) 'Eternally condemned' is a strong phrase both in Greek (*anathema*) and in its Hebrew equivalent (*herem*). It means something utterly devoted to destruction, like the Old Testament city of Jericho. Achan, however, thought otherwise, took some of the forbidden booty and brought destruction on himself and his family (Josh. 7). He was 'anathematised', he fell under the curse of God. Likewise, says Paul, if anyone perverts the gospel, he too is under divine judgment.

Some commentators have suggested that this is a very harsh comment and Paul was more than a little carried away with his own rhetoric. However, that is not an option: he repeats himself in the very next verse. Others mitigate the force of his language by reminding us that Paul was a child of his age or that he failed to show consistently the true spirit of his Master, Jesus, at this point. In other words, we create a wedge between the apostle and the Lord. But this ignores the issue, which is one of truth. Did not the Lord Jesus himself, love incarnate, warn of error in equally frightening terms? For instance, he said, 'If anyone causes one of these little ones who believe in me to sin, it would be better for him to be thrown into the sea with a large millstone tied round his neck' (Mk. 9:42).

Such words jar in the ears of a society that believes we can make up our own truth as we go along. But think of it like this. The gospel is God's ozone layer of grace. It shuts out the harmful effects of God's wrath on sin. False teaching is like the carbon emissions which create holes in the ozone layer. False teaching is dangerous. It suggests that human merit, personal performance, law-keeping etc are all necessary to salvation. The effect is to puncture holes in God's grace, exposing us to the searing rays of God's judgment. Paul knows that such heat would eternally condemn us. It is only the good news of Jesus that can save us, since it is neither 'man made' (v11), nor did the apostle receive it from anybody else but Jesus (v12). So the gospel is bigger than Paul, it is greater than the messenger. That's why he is so inclusive: 'even if we' or 'an angel' or 'anybody' (vs 8,9) pervert the gospel, such are liable to judgment.

That Christians are called to be Christlike, even when they disagree with others, is a given. But we are not called simply to be so 'nice' that we fear to upset others who have a different gospel. I think it is particularly interesting that the apostle even includes 'an angel.' Two major post-Christian faiths claim angelic authority for their revelations. For instance, Islam claims to be the religion that supersedes Christianity. It teaches that the angel Gabriel gave Mohammed a different story to the one we have now in the New Testament. It affirms the virgin birth of Jesus, accords him the status of a great prophet but denies that Jesus died on the cross, much less for our sins, and therefore denies his resurrection that affirms that he is uniquely God's Son. Similarly, *The Book of Mormon* gives us another gospel to believe, one revealed by the angel Moroni, the son of Mormon, to Joseph Smith in 1823. But there is one test for the messenger and his message: do they faithfully bring the message of Jesus Christ? Isaiah 8:20 gives us the yardstick: 'If they do not speak according to this word, they have no light of dawn.'

Does this sound a little intolerant? If my grandson, Daniel, tells me he has learned that two plus two equals five, I'm intolerant: 'Dan, that isn't true.' If we are not intolerant about some things, we cannot be Christians. It was Jesus who claimed, 'I am the way, and the truth and the life. No-one comes to the Father except through me' (Jn. 14:6). I believe him. The Early Church seemed to think so too: 'there is no other name . . . by which we must be saved' (Acts 4:12). That is not going to answer all my questions and settle all my problems about other faiths, but it commits me to Jesus and therefore not others as the way to God.

- *How harmful is it when we water down the gospel in a way that Paul (and Jesus) did not? Discuss ways we tend to 'sanitise' the gospel to make it more palatable for non-believers.*
- *How would you share the gospel (with special reference to Jn. 14:6) with someone who told you confidently that 'All paths lead to God, so it doesn't matter what you believe'? Role-play such a scenario in twos.*

CHRISTIANS CAN BE DIVERTED

Why is Paul so intolerant concerning the truth of Jesus? Simply because Christians can be turned away from Christ, the Lord who has done all that is necessary to bring us into God's family. In the Galatian churches, the congregations were being persuaded that this was just not enough: 'You've still got to get to grips with God's law, to start to take on its obligations, especially circumcision' seems to have been the false teachers' mantra. To anticipate chapter 3 of this letter, there Paul will remind these believers that the gospel of Jesus was always God's first plan, Plan A.

Through it he intended to bless the world (3:8). Plan B, the law, had a different purpose and function, as we will see (3:19). With the coming of Jesus everything is now different, the New Age has dawned to deliver us from 'the present evil age' (v4). What the whole of the Old Testament was straining towards and foreshadowing has arrived through all that Jesus represents and has accomplished. When we are trusting Christ, we need neither the law, nor anyone or anything else, to save us. He does that completely (Heb. 7:25). Yet these Galatians were in danger of deserting the very Jesus who had saved them.

No wonder Paul is 'astonished' by their desertion (v6). The Galatians were not getting an improved gospel, something of the same type. No, it was 'different', a strong word meaning the very opposite of the 'same gospel' (we use part of the word in the term '*hetero*sexual'– attracted to the *opposite* sex). In fact, they were in danger of becoming deserters, a word used to describe someone who leaves one political party to join another one, or of an army deserter, guilty of treachery in the face of the enemy. In changing their opinions, in swapping sides, these converts were about to kiss goodbye to God's salvation. They, in effect, were saying farewell to Jesus. And what would be the result? 'Peace', as in verse 3? It was the very opposite: 'confusion' (v7), trouble, a word that is used to describe the kind of terror the disciples felt when they thought they were seeing a ghost walking on the Lake of Galilee (Mt. 14:26). False teaching can simultaneously boil our brains whilst freezing our hearts to the Lord Jesus, via a ceaseless round of perpetual obligation in which our best is never good enough.

We must not miss the importance of this point. These converts were not simply changing their opinions or deserting a doctrine they once believed. No, they were 'deserting the one who called you' (v6), God himself. It's fashionable (and very post-modern!) to drive a wedge between God and the Bible. But if I turn from the gospel, it is from God himself that I turn. Then I discover that I am left to my own resources. By contrast, the gospel is about living in the grace of God, not my own power: 'Christ lives in me!' (2:20).

Are you going through a crisis of faith or a trauma at the moment? Do you wonder whether the gospel and all it offers in Christ is enough? Indeed, that scene I referred to in Matthew 14, the storm on the lake, may picture just how we feel: we're in a storm! Other gospels offer us solutions that bring anything but calm. In contrast, in the gospel, I hear Jesus say, 'Take courage! It is I. Don't be afraid' (Mt. 14:27). Peace indeed. Sound theology, the gospel, glues us together because it ensures we stick to Christ. It is therefore well worth defending, no matter whom we fail to please. That was certainly Paul's experience, as verse 10 illustrates.

● *How can tweaking the gospel in what seems to be a small way – perhaps by just adding one ingredient – change it to something completely different?*

THE TRUTH MUST BE ASSERTED

The false teachers, it seems, were playing a clever game with the Galatians. They suggested that the apostle Paul had not told the Galatians the whole truth: his gospel was a cut-price affair, designed to make him popular among them. It left out the important bits about the law and the like. So, they asserted, when he was with the Jews, he preached one message: when he was with the Gentiles, he preached another. Really? If the Galatians had survived Paul's exocet missiles of gospel truth in verses 6-9, one can almost see a wry smile on Paul's face as he rebuts the charge of currying human favour: 'Am I now trying to win the approval of men, or of God? Or am I trying to please men? If I were still trying to please men, I would not be a servant of Christ' (v10).

There are, sad to say, chameleon-like Christian leaders who do adapt to the environment they are in. It was said of a certain minister: 'He was at our church ten years and he never upset anybody.' What a terrible judgement! If I stand by the gospel of Jesus, I am going to upset some people. It must not be my personal offensiveness, of course, but 'the offence of the cross' (5:11). John Wesley, one of the founding fathers of Methodism, once asked one of his local preachers how his preaching had fared the day before. After a rather bland reply, Wesley pressed him: 'Did you make anyone glad?' 'No,' he said. 'Did you make anyone sad?' 'No.' In exasperation, Wesley asked, 'Did you make anyone mad?' 'No.' 'Then why didn't you just stay in bed, man?' Wesley responded. The New English Bible translates verse 10 as follows: 'Does my language sound as if I were canvassing for men's support? Whose support do I want but God's alone?' If it is a choice between pleasing people and pleasing God by staying loyal to the gospel, then the choice is clear.

We are living in a period when many in the western world find it hard to understand that someone may have firm convictions. Tolerance is supposedly the great virtue, so we cannot afford to tolerate intolerance. Take religious convictions: many people cannot understand the sense of outrage that ran through the Islamic communities worldwide in 2006 over the production of some Danish cartoons, which many Muslims felt demeaned their prophet Mohammed. But committed Christians should be able to understand their feelings, for we too are people of conviction, committed to truth. However, Paul isn't about to despatch any first century death squads to sort out the false teachers; rather, he will appeal to the churches on the basis of 'the truth of the gospel' (2:14).

We could subtitle verses 6-10 'How not to win friends and influence people.' Of course, like us all, Paul was glad, I suspect, to have people's approval and, just now and again, the appreciation of his converts. Who does not want to live at peace with everyone if at all possible? But he would not sacrifice the gospel on the altar of human approval and so displease God.

- *Have you ever had people sneer at you because of your faith? How did it affect your confidence in sharing your faith when further opportunities arose?*
- *Is it harder to share your faith with someone you know well, or a stranger?*

Whom are we trying to please ultimately? It's said that when one of Verdi's operas was being premiered in Milan, he stood in the wings and was oblivious to all the cheers and applause of the audience. He was not at all concerned about who was pleased with his opera, with one exception, one of his inspirational predecessors, the great Rossini. Would he applaud, for his approval meant more than all the crowd combined? Our lives would be far less stressed and free of so many fears and doubts, if we could but learn to play for the only One whose opinion ultimately matters: the Lord who made us and bought us.

Josef Tson, a pastor who suffered regular interrogation and imprisonment for his faith during Romania's communist regime, testifies that a little rhyme kept him going in tough times. It went something like this:

I'll look to my God and say,
'Father, are you pleased with me?'
He'll look down on me and say,
'Son, you got the victory.'

All that will matter one day is whether we have pleased 'the audience of One', and hear his 'Well done, son, daughter. You got the victory!'

FURTHER STUDY

Read about Daniel in the lions' den (Dan. 6). Daniel put himself at risk by behaving as he did. But then, he had already shown himself to be a bold character (Dan. 1:8). Without a doubt, he put God first. Of course, it is not always easy to put into practice. But that is what our God requires.

REFLECTION AND RESPONSE

- 'Are you going through a crisis of faith or a personal trauma at the moment? Do you wonder whether the gospel and all it offers in Christ is enough?' Is that true of you right now? Spend some time before God.

- In our present culture, tolerance is a must-have virtue. How far can Christians truly be tolerant, especially when faced with beliefs and attitudes we know deny the truth? How important is it for *you* to please 'the audience of One'?

- Ask God for boldness in telling others about his Son, and trust him to give you courage and wisdom in every situation you will face this week.

SMALL GROUP DISCUSSION POINT

Share any experiences you have had when you have taken a risk to share your faith. If you have never taken a risk, share that too! Spend some time praying for each other, for boldness and a new desire to tell others about Jesus.

CHAPTER 3

Unexpected grace

GALATIANS 1:11-24

Aim: To see the importance of 'the divine side' of testimony

FOCUS ON THE THEME
Strike a match and see if you can give your testimony before you burn your fingers. If you don't have a match, set yourself a minute and a half and see if you can give a complete testimony before the time runs out!

Reading: Galatians 1:11-24
Key verses: Galatians 1:12,23,24

In a local church setting some years ago, I regularly trained fellow Christians to share their testimony very briefly in the way described above. The trainees would strike a match and had to give their story before they got their fingers burnt. How did they manage it in perhaps thirty seconds? Answer: we would work BC/AD. I would encourage them to mention one area of life Before Christ, how they came to faith, and then the difference Christ makes, life AD. Such sessions were often great fun but the purpose was always serious: how to put in a good word for Jesus when other arguments failed.

In this section, Paul uses his testimony to defend himself against the charge that he was not a fully-fledged apostle, because he had either received the gospel from others or somehow corrupted it. Still today similar charges are levelled at him. Lord Beaverbrook, once a well-known newspaper proprietor, spoke for many when he stated that Paul was 'incapable by nature of understanding the spirit of the Master.' A long line of critics have seen him as the arch corrupter of the 'simple message of Jesus.' Was he? On the contrary, Paul tells us here: 'The gospel I preached is not something that man made up' (v11): literally, 'is not according to man' or 'no human invention' (JBP).[1] Rather, his gospel was 'from Jesus Christ' (v12). But simply 'sayin' it don't make it so', according to Huckleberry Finn. So Paul used his testimony BC/AD to back up his claim that he was preaching the original, authentic gospel of Jesus.

BC – THE PERSECUTOR (13,14)

Before he was a Christian, Paul was simultaneously famous and infamous: infamous as a persecutor of the Church (v13) and famous for his zeal and commitment to Judaism (v14). So far as Christianity was concerned, he saw himself as Judaism's inquisitor general, the man to stamp it out. His persecutions were carried out 'intensely'; his aim was 'to destroy' the Church, a strong word used elsewhere for the destruction of a whole city. He hated Christianity. Why? His loathing was fed by his intense commitment to Judaism, 'outstripping many of my Jewish contemporaries' (JBP). Elsewhere we learn of his background: born in Tarsus but educated 'under Gamaliel' (Acts 22:3), the most famous Jewish teacher of his time. While Gamaliel himself was far more cautious in his reaction to the Christian faith (Acts 5:33-40), Paul, with 'fanatical zeal' (JBP) sought Christianity's demise. There was nothing in his background to suggest that he was ripe for conversion. His point runs something like this: if I didn't get the gospel from Judaism because I was so deeply entrenched in it, and didn't receive it from Christians because I was at war with them, what brought about the change? The answer: 'It pleased God' (v15 RSV).

● *Do you have any friends or family that are 'anti-God' as opposed to not being interested? Praise God that he is the One who changes people and situations and pray for them.*

THE TURNING POINT – THE CONVERT (15,16)

So often when we hear stories of conversion, the emphasis falls on the human element: I had a Christian home; a friend shared Christ with me; I attended an Alpha Course; I read the Bible; I accepted Jesus; I saw it made sense; I decided to become a Christian. Here Paul emphasises the divine side. It was God who took the initiative, who 'set me apart from birth and called me by his grace' (v15). The details of Paul's conversion are well known, the 'Damascus Road' experience (Acts 9). Scholars have debated the origin of Paul's gospel *ad nauseam*. How did a first century Pharisee become the greatest Christian missionary? How did he come to see that a discredited impostor – a crucified Messiah! – was, in a unique sense, the 'Son of God' (v16, 4:4), and the fulfilment of all God's purposes in space and time (Col. 1:15-20)? I suspect, if anyone – sceptical scholars included – had met the risen Jesus as Paul had, then in an instant anyone's theology would be revolutionised. Does any of this apply generally to 'ordinary' Christians? Certainly.

Real conversion is a hugely divine affair. It started with God in *eternity* before we were born (v15 and cf Jer. 1:5 and Is. 49:1, Eph. 1:4); in *time*, we respond to Christ's call (Mt. 11:28-30); and in *experience*, we receive 'his Son' (v16). Sadly, too many public testimonies are strong on the lurid details of the 'BC', mention 'his Son in me' as the climax and then splutter to a stop; not so Paul's testimony.

● *Think about your testimony – from the 'divine side.' Can you see how God engineered events, people, meetings and so on, to bring you to him?*

AD – THE PREACHER (17-24)

Many older Christians were raised on the slogan 'Saved to Serve.' It is very biblical. For Paul, that service involved 'preaching', a term used a number of times in this chapter (vs 8,9,11,16,23). It is literally the word 'evangelise.' For him, the good news sharing about Jesus was to be primarily amongst Gentiles (v16). Many of his Galatian believers had been all that implied: 'Christless', 'stateless', 'promiseless', 'hopeless' and 'godless', as William Hendricksen has brilliantly summarised Ephesians 2:12. However his mission got under way, Paul needed time and space for reflection and preparation. I am persuaded that a period of 'up to three years' was Paul's equivalent to the other apostles' three years on earth with Jesus, though it may have been shorter (Acts 9:20-25).

One of my privileges, as a Bible college principal, is meeting with people, young and old, anxious to serve the Lord. It is not always easy to persuade some that a period of formal preparation through a college is anything but a diversion from the main work of evangelism. A moment's reflection, however, challenges that notion. When I board a jet, I hope the pilots have been thoroughly trained for every eventuality on the flight, even if only in a simulator. If a surgeon's going to perform open-heart surgery on me, I am comforted to know she has performed the procedure hundreds of times, rather than having just completed a basic first aid course. Gospel ministry seeks to 'fly' people from this world to the next and to expose them to the most radical heart surgery – a new one (Ezek. 36:26). Therefore gospel 'ministers' need to be equally competent. As Billy Graham is reported to have said, 'If I only had three years available to serve the Lord, I would spend two of them in study and preparation.'

All that said, the main point in the apostle's argument here is this: I did not get the gospel second-hand, 'I did not consult any man' (v16). Rather, when he was converted, Paul firstly needed *privacy* (v17) and certainly not the *publicity* that an immediate visit to Jerusalem might have given (v18). 'But, hang on a moment Paul, you did go to Jerusalem', says an objector, 'and we suspect you got your gospel there' (Acts 9:26-29). 'Hardly,' would be an apt response. First, there was the sheer *brevity* of his visit – a couple of weeks, whose purpose was to 'get acquainted with Peter' (v18) not the gospel. Secondly, it was three years after his conversion, when he had already started preaching and was actually 'unknown by face' (literal translation), in Judea, 'personally unknown' (v22). He could have been known as 'Paul the obscure.' What did go before him, however, was something far more telling than his personal presence. It was the story of his amazing turnaround: 'the man who formerly persecuted is now preaching the faith he once tried to destroy' (v23).

There was nothing bland about Paul's conversion and testimony. Because of Jesus he had turned 180 degrees. There's always something special when we hear the testimony of someone who's gone through an equally radical conversion from an unlikely background: a witch who comes to Christ, a murderer who is converted in prison, a religious leader who forsakes his gods and turns to Jesus. Once again, however, Paul is seeking to make a huge point in his defence. Far from his inventing the gospel, the reason the churches of Judea praised God for him (v24) had one major cause: he was 'now preaching the faith' (v23). Notice that phrase, *the faith*. It means the same gospel as they believed in Judea and Jerusalem. Was Paul the arch corrupter of the simple message of Jesus? Preposterous!

● *What testimony books have you read and what impact have they had on you? Which ones would you want to lend to others?*

CONCLUSION

I recently received a replacement credit card similar to the one I had, save that the start and expiry dates had changed. All the other details were the same. The details were fairly easy to check because if I placed one card on top of the other, following the indentations in the plastic made by my name and numbers, the two cards fitted together, as if they belonged to each other. Likewise, Paul seems to invite us to see if his new credit card fits snugly with the old credit card of the apostolic gospel. There are always 'conspiracy theorists' that think it doesn't, without any historical evidence to back up their wild claims. Paul's point is that his gospel could be historically verified by those who were his contemporaries. He puts it plainly: 'I assure you before God that what I am writing to you is no lie' (v20). What do you believe about the origin and truth of the gospel Paul preached? I believe Paul's account. Why? Because these are the facts, the truth of the matter. To return to my opening paragraph's illustration of boxes of matches and testimonies, when I ignore truth, I might get more than my fingers get burned!

FURTHER STUDY

Read the story of Zacchaeus in Luke 19:1-9. How did this tax collector prove to Jesus and others that a real change had taken place in his heart?

REFLECTION AND RESPONSE

- Paul was an unlikely convert because he was already deeply committed to his faith. In your experience, are religious people harder to convert than the outright godless? Why do you think that is? Think about the reasons and pray for anyone you know who you feel might have 'religion' but lack real relationship with Christ, that they will meet him and know the joy of his presence.

- Think about Paul's amazing change of heart and life, and the testimonies of others you know that have completed a U-turn when they have met Christ. Be encouraged by the awesomeness and power of God . . . the same God who lives in you by his Spirit.

- It's not easy to believe that someone can be changed. Do you know anyone from a challenging background who has become a Christian, and who may be struggling in some way to overcome their past reputation? Encourage them this week.

SMALL GROUP DISCUSSION POINT

Think of ways to improve the preparation of Christian leaders, for example, the need for time, reflection and study, as suggested by Paul's Arabian experience (v17). This can be carried out at all levels of your church: Sunday school, youth work, eldership etc. And for yourself – how can you improve your own preparation for Christian service, in whatever situation Jesus calls you? Brainstorm in twos or threes, and then share your thoughts and ideas.

CHAPTER 4

Know your enemy and your friends

GALATIANS 2:1-10

Aim: To keep focused on 'the main thing' – the new creation in Christ.

FOCUS ON THE THEME:
'I knew something was wrong when the new pastor decided that certain methods of Eastern meditation should be included in our prayer meetings. Then he told us that it wasn't necessary to believe Jesus actually rose from the dead and that the Spirit of God was a "concept". I had to leave. The guy just wasn't preaching Christ Jesus, crucified and risen, and the need to be born again by the Spirit of God.' But how easy is it to walk out of a situation like this where people you've known and trusted for a long time seem to see things differently to you?

Reading: Galatians 2:1-10
Key verses: Galatians 2:2a,9a

I was quizzing an American pastor friend about the secret, humanly speaking, of the growth of his church from a few dozen to some seven thousand members over the last thirty years. 'Steve,' he replied 'the main thing is to keep the main thing, the main thing!' For him, that meant he kept plugging away, year in year out, at sharing the gospel of

Jesus as faithfully and as frequently as he and his members could.

In this passage we're confronted by the 'main thing.' From the outside, Christianity presents a bewildering array of ecclesiastical options: bishops/overseers are necessary/unnecessary; women should/should not be allowed to be priests; worship styles should be contemporary/only traditional, etc. In this section of the letter, Paul is once again defending his position. His opponents' argument seems to run like this: 'Don't you know Paul was called to Jerusalem and on the carpet for his defective gospel? In fact, the Gentile Titus, we hear, was circumcised, so proving our point: you need the "full gospel" that we Jewish Christians have.' Paul speaks biographically. When people are prejudiced and have got hold of the wrong end of the stick, facts act as a reality check. Abraham Maslow once said that for a man whose only tool is a hammer, every problem is a nail. Paul has many other tools, but here he does hammer home three 'nails' to prove that there's only one real gospel – and he and the other apostles both shared and preached it. On the 'main thing' they were united.

NAIL ONE – COMPANIONS (1-3)

Paul's opponents knew he had been to Jerusalem 'fourteen years later' (v1). That is either the visit of Acts 11:30 or 15:1-4: one a famine relief visit, the other the so-called Council of Jerusalem. One of his two companions' credentials were impeccable. Barnabas, 'the son of encouragement', the man with the 'biggest heart in the church' (Acts 4:36; 9:27; 11:24), was Jewish through and through, *kosher* we might say. Not so Titus: he was an uncircumcised Greek (v3). So Paul undoubtedly used Titus's presence as both a test case – would the Jerusalem leadership and church accept him? –

and a powerful testimony to the gospel's effects. Acts 15:12 speaks of the 'miraculous signs and wonders' performed among the Gentiles that silenced the critics of Gentile evangelism. Titus was a living 'sign and wonder' of the grace of God – *without being circumcised.*

It's easy to imagine that the foregoing has little to say to today's world. Far from it. The issue then was, does a Gentile have to become a Jew in order to be a Christian? Now it can be, does a Catholic have to become a Protestant, or vice-versa, to become a Christian? Can I be a real Christian if I do/don't belong to that particular church? As Paul will summarise it, 'Neither circumcision nor uncircumcision means anything; what counts is a new creation' (6:15). At the end of certain mathematical equations, as a teenager, I recall the need to add 'QED' – *quod erat demonstrandum* – 'that which was to be proved.' Both Barnabas and Titus were now 'new creations.' Circumcision could not be essential – QED.

In addition to Paul's 'living exhibits', there are two other 'prongs' to this nail. First, Paul's visit to Jerusalem was not occasioned by his being called to account: the Lord told him to go, via 'revelation' (perhaps via the prophecy of Acts 11:28). Secondly, when Paul arrived he gave a 'full exposition of the gospel I preach' (JBP). Notice the tense of the verb, 'I am (still) preaching, continue to preach.' What he was preaching before he went to Jerusalem, he continued thereafter to preach. There had been no additions, no change to the basic 'truth of the gospel' (v5). Does that sound boring?

Dr Billy Graham has been an evangelist for over sixty years. He would be the first to say that the heart of his message is still the same. Of course, as he and any *mature* Christian has discovered, one's appreciation of the greatness of the gospel – its coherence, implications, applications and its astonishing relevance to every part of life in this world – should grow. Paul elsewhere speaks of the 'unsearchable riches of Christ' (Eph. 3:8). Here it is 'the truth of the gospel' (v5). How very profound!

There is one further point to note from this section. Paul did this primary presentation 'privately' to fellow 'leaders', because he did not want his work to be 'in vain' (v2). The last phrase almost certainly has to do with the type of situation the infant Gentile churches faced from the hardline Jewish Christians: 'Unless you are circumcised . . . you cannot be saved' (Acts 15:1). If the Judaisers' notions had prevailed, ultimately Christianity would have remained a mere sect of Judaism and have perished in the first decades of its existence. Paul's manoeuvre is smart. He needs the other apostolic church leaders on board, for there are issues that everyone in a church should know about. Some issues require mature leadership's discussion, reflection and decision. After that, as appropriate, everyone else in the church can be involved. However, theological and church issues are rarely resolved so easily in the first or the twenty-first century, as Nail Two makes clear.

● *How has your appreciation of the gospel grown since you became a Christian? What excites you most at the moment?*

NAIL TWO – INFILTRATORS (4,5)

The grammar of this section is a little difficult, very possibly because Paul, as he relates this incident, is still feeling very emotionally charged. Perhaps a garbled version of events was being hawked around by these 'false brothers' (v4) to the effect that the real discussion centred on one big issue: why wasn't Titus circumcised? Maybe one or two high-placed Christian leaders felt some sympathy for what could be viewed as a 'measure of prudence.' After all, didn't Paul do something similar in the case of Timothy (Acts 16:3)?

Paul does not mince his words. Literally, he calls them 'pseudo-brothers': a 'fifth column' of spies and traitors who had 'wormed their way into our meeting' (JBP). Their purpose was altogether sinister. Let's take a step back to feel the full force of the issues at stake.

Here Paul talks of 'the freedom we have in Christ' (v4). The Lord Jesus himself had promised 'If the Son sets you free, you will be free indeed', a freedom linked to knowing the truth that sets us free (Jn. 8:36,32). Later, Paul will remind these Galatians that 'It is for freedom that Christ has set us free' (5:1). The freedom envisaged, of course, is that ultimate deliverance from sin, corruption and evil in both the world at large and the human heart in particular that the death and resurrection of Jesus have addressed. So we 'never boast except in the cross of our Lord Jesus Christ' (6:14) because through it 'we may be justified by faith in Christ and not by observing the law' (2:16).

These infiltrators, however, had another agenda, 'to make us slaves' (v4). Paul's reaction was that 'We did not give these men an inch' (JBP). And with whom did the Jerusalem leadership side? They 'gave me and Barnabas the right hand of fellowship' (v9). In other words, the apostles stood together, not breaking ranks, because they were united in this 'truth of the gospel.' Was Paul the arch-corrupter of the Christian faith, peddling an inferior, cut-price gospel? No way!

In many parts of the world today, Christians know first-hand about false brothers who infiltrate their ranks to distort the gospel and enslave the church. Consider the experience of many believers under twentieth century Soviet communism. In other parts of the church, the infiltration is more subtle but just as dangerous. There are church members and leaders who do not believe the 'truth of the gospel' and slowly and insidiously introduce another gospel (1:8) that dethrones Christ as Lord and substitutes a 'way of salvation' that simply means 'Christ died for nothing' (2:21). Christians are called to be as wide as the gospel, welcoming all as family who, despite all other differences, 'belong to Christ' (3:29f). Christians are to be as narrow as the gospel, excluding that which is false since it enslaves (4:9). Finally, there's a third nail.

● *Whether it's another doctrine, trusting in works or even in another person (such as a leader), 'another gospel' can creep in to even the most sound church. How can we ensure we aren't being slowly led off track?*

NAIL THREE – PARTNERS

Some people like to put Christian leaders on pedestals, boost their credentials to mega-star status, then quote them as authorities, as if they personally knew them. Such people often have their own agenda to control and intimidate the unwary. Something like this seems to be the target for Paul's somewhat dismissive statements concerning apostolic leadership in Jerusalem: 'seemed to be leaders' (v2), 'seemed to be important' (v6) 'reputed (lit: 'seemed') to be pillars' (v9).

Whether people are 'leaders', 'important' or 'pillars' in the local church, the real test of anyone's position is allegiance to the good news of Jesus. Leaders are called to be faithful to the gospel. Sometimes they themselves are strangers to its power. For instance, an evangelist had just finished preaching in a Baptist church in the USA. One man in the congregation looked particularly disturbed and disagreeable. So, as the opportunity presented itself, the evangelist asked him kindly, 'Do you want to become a Christian, friend?' The man was outraged and snarled, 'I've been a deacon in this church for over twenty-five years!'

'Oh, don't let that stop you!' replied the evangelist. Nicodemus was 'Israel's teacher' but still needed to be 'born again' (Jn. 3:5-10).

In truth, these apostles were vitally important leaders, pillars of the church. And every local church needs such leadership. Over the years, I've observed 'pillars' in many local churches, people who are stable, steadfast and deeply rooted in God. Every church needs such leaders.

Paul's purpose in mentioning these leaders is critical. For they perceived that God was equally at work, literally 'energising' both Peter and Paul, for gospel work among Jews and Gentiles respectively (v8). Naturally, this 'division of labour' was not watertight. We only need to read Acts to see Peter being used to bring a Gentile, Cornelius, to Christ and Paul reaching Jews (Acts 10; 13:42-43). After all, the Lord's commission was and still is the gospel to 'all nations' (Mt. 28:18-20). That said, even apostles had specific emphases in their evangelism. Thank God for those who are contemporary specialists in reaching people defined by different religious, cultural or racial markers. Sometimes missionaries spend years learning how best to tell the good news so that it sounds like it is good news. 'Contextualisation' is the jargon word: ask any missionary for details. Such people need our prayers and support in the great missionary task and challenge of the church – that 'all may be one in Christ' (Gal. 3:28).

● *We all have different gifts and should share the gospel where we can, as the Lord gives us opportunities. But some are rightly called to be evangelists – 'specialists' in different parts of the world, or working amongst diverse people groups. How can we more effectively support their often gruelling and isolating work?*

The result of the apostolic recognition that God was at work is the seemingly innocuous phrase, 'gave me and Barnabas the right hand of fellowship' (v9). Anyone who has followed the conflict in the Middle East or the tensions in Northern Irish politics immediately recognises that such a gesture may speak ten thousand words. Between Peter, James, John and Paul, following the traditional ascriptions of authorship, we have at least twenty-one of the twenty-seven books of our New Testament accounted for, and at least three other books by close apostolic association. Within the pages of those apostolic documents is found food for thought and the soul, and life for the world. Thank God for an apostolic faith preserved in the pages of our Bibles.

FURTHER STUDY

In Revelation 2:1-3 we see Jesus commending the church for testing those 'who claim to be apostles but are not.' Paul was firm in his setting out of the gospel he preached to the Gentiles. Some agendas aren't always so clear. How can we tell what agendas preachers and teachers are following?

REFLECTION AND RESPONSE

- A thief who had never been baptised or walked a step to follow Jesus nevertheless joined him in Paradise. He had nothing to commend him but a total trust in Jesus. How does this encourage/challenge you?

- Pray for anyone you know who doesn't fit the mould but is certainly a new creation in Christ. How can you best help them to grow in their faith?

- Pray for the pillars in your church, that they may have discernment in determining the enemies of the flock who might cause disruption. Pray that the leaders would stay true to Christ, united in their allegiance to the gospel.

SMALL GROUP DISCUSSION POINT
Share testimonies of grace where someone who didn't look or sound the part blessed you in some way. Include any testimonies you may have read in books or magazines, or speakers who have come to your church.

CHAPTER 5

How to stay up when a leader lets you down

GALATIANS 2:11-14

Aim: To understand that it is right to challenge leadership when necessary

---

FOCUS ON THE THEME:
Do the critical test. How do you respond to personal criticism?
a) Seethe with fury and have to repent before the Lord?
b) Stiffly inform them that it is sinful to criticize anyone and you are only answerable to God?
c) Cry, 'Bless you brother/sister. I needed to know that! Please feel free to point out any other flaws in my character!' and mean it?
How easy do you think it is to give or take criticism – especially when dealing with leadership?

Reading: Galatians 2:11-14
Key verse: Galatians 2:11

At first sight this passage seems to have little to say to our contemporary world. Within the argument of Galatians, of course, it was vital to put the record straight. Paul's opponents would have seized on this very public bust-up with Peter and used it to suggest that the fall-out was over the nature of the gospel which, they'd have said, Peter had right and Paul wrong. If it were reported today in a quality newspaper, we would expect a headline such as: 'Church debates the boundaries of communion', whilst a tabloid would run with something like: 'Ecclesiastical punch-up at Antioch: Bishop-bashing Paul screams, "Pete, you got it wrong!"'

What about contemporary headlines? A while ago *The Times* carried two articles on the advice and behaviour of a couple of clergymen. The first, a 75 year old priest in North London, was advocating shoplifting from 'evil superstores', as he termed them: 'It's not stealing, but a badly needed reallocation of economic resources.' The second, a pastor in South London, was gaoled for stealing £56,000 from, of all things, a *police* bank account!

Every Christian should be aware that leaders have feet of clay. I think of an older man, sexually abused in a Christian orphanage, carrying the emotional scars over fifty years on, still unable to form long-term relationships. I'm reminded of a teenage boy shattered because his Dad went off with another woman. I have recently counselled one of my students here at Moorlands as he comes to terms with the life sentence imposed on his own pastor for sexual offences against young boys. Some clear lessons for today's leaders and Church emerge from this section.

SOME LEADERS CAN BE HYPOCRITICAL

Various financial investment adverts carry a warning to the effect that past performance is no guarantee of future growth. No-one could ever doubt Peter's past performance from the Day of Pentecost onwards: bold as a lion in his preaching, fearless before the religious authorities, wise in his delegation of responsibilities and open to the Spirit to cross religious and cultural barriers for the gospel (Acts chapters 2;4;6;10). The latter incident is especially pertinent here. In his going to the home of the Gentile Cornelius, sharing the gospel with 'a large gathering of people' and witnessing how 'the Holy Spirit came' (Acts 10:27,44), Peter had taken one giant step for the Kingdom of God. Those initially cautious, when they heard the facts, praised God because he had 'granted even the Gentiles repentance to life' (Acts 11:2,3,18). The Church had been launched on an irrevocable journey: it would not remain a sect of Judaism but fulfil its calling to be the place where 'Jew and Greek, slave and free' could be the one family of God (3:28).

How was such unity expressed? In the Early Church, eating together, 'table fellowship', would culminate in remembering the Lord's sacrifice for them (1 Cor. 11:17-34). Peter was clearly happy to join in: he used to eat with the Gentiles (v12). After all, it was the death of the Lord Jesus that made both Jew and Gentile the one people of God (Eph. 2:13f). Clearly, Peter believed that. He knew the gospel was for all nations (Mt. 8:11, 28:19f). He never stopped *believing* it. He just stopped *behaving* it. Instead of 'acting in line with the truth of the gospel' (v14) he was 'play acting', the meaning of 'hypocrisy' (v13). Indeed, the very way the words are used, 'began to draw back and separate himself from the Gentiles' (v12), suggests something sly, surreptitious and gradual. He would just miss a meal here and there until his absence would not be too noticeable.

We don't know what precise message, or garbled version of it, the 'certain men' brought from James (v11). Perhaps it was something along the lines of 'Peter, word on the street in Jerusalem is that you've apostatised from your Jewish roots. And the result is pressure and persecution on Jewish Christians, especially in Judea.' After all, Paul himself knew such reactions, as this letter indicates (5:11, 6:12), and is illustrated repeatedly in Acts (e.g. 21:28). It must have been really heavy pressure, for the lion-hearted Peter 'was afraid', intimidated by the 'circumcision group' (v12).

We should never underestimate the power of pressure groups, in and outside the church, to make a leader pliable to their dictates. Sometimes they may question the leader's orthodoxy, as seemingly here, or whether they are truly open to God. Some leaders buckle under the pressure of the raised eyebrow of disapproval or yield to the temptation to be popular and viewed as 'really in touch with where it's at', whatever that particular fashion or whim may be. The results can be devastating. In Peter's case, it threatened the unity of the Church and the integrity of the gospel. How do we know it was serious? The poignant phrase 'even Barnabas was led astray' says it all. The big-hearted 'son of encouragement' (Acts 4:36), who had rejoiced over Gentiles finding Christ (Acts 11:23), now joined the cast of this hypocritical drama being acted out with the 'other Jews' (v13).

Again there's an important principle here. When a leader falls, they may take others down with them. Most Christians know people who were once interested in the gospel, were church members, or even leaders, who are no longer active in their faith because they were let down by a minister, youth leader, Sunday School teacher etc. Religious profession, when mixed with hypocrisy, is highly toxic and can lead to God's name being dishonoured (check out Romans 2:17-24, the last verse particularly). The antidote? In this passage one in particular is given, though there are others, depending on the precise circumstances of the problem. When a leader fails other leaders must help.

● *What can be done to help those affected by the failure of a leader? Brainstorm some ideas.*

OTHER LEADERS NEED TO STAY FAITHFUL

A distinguishing mark of an outstanding leader is not merely to see things but see through things to their implications. Paul was such a leader. The result of Peter's public withdrawal from 'table fellowship' with Gentiles would inevitably lead to major schism: two tables, two communions, two churches, Jewish and Gentile versions, rather than one Church of neither 'Greek or Jew, circumcised or uncircumcised' where 'Christ is all, and is in all' (Col. 3:11). After all, it was at Antioch that great numbers of people had come to the Lord, and where the word 'Christians', for the first time, had been used to describe this astonishing amalgam of Jewish and Gentile believers in Jesus (Acts 11:26). Significant too is the fact that Antioch was to become the great missionary church to the world (Acts 13:1-3). Peter's behaviour threatened everything, the very future of the Church as we know it. If the 'Judaisers', to give the 'certain men' their technical title, had their way, then every Gentile would have been following a Jewish diet, undergoing (male) circumcision, upholding the Sabbath and simply becoming Jews. That would be to turn the clock back to 'BC', before Christ had died and risen from the dead to be 'Lord of all' (Acts 10:36). The Judaisers did not know the time! Paul did: time to confront Peter.

Paul's confrontation with Peter was both personal, 'I opposed him to his face' (v11), and public, 'I said to Peter in front of them all' (v14). It was personal, for Paul did not merely mutter away about the problem to others, running Peter down but not having the guts to face him. That happens too often in both the Church and world at large. It was necessarily public since Peter's behaviour was in the public domain. The implications of Peter's actions were that Gentile believers were second-class, not 'quite there'

Christians. The gospel says something entirely different, as the next section (vs 15-21) will underline. So Paul stays loyal to the gospel and opposes Peter.

I expect some may be wondering why Paul did not just have a little private chat with the offender. After all, Paul describes something like that later in the epistle (6:1). Doesn't 'Dr' Jesus prescribe certain remedies for conflict resolution in the gospels (Mt. 18:15-17)? This highlights some of the principles of what is called church discipline. Generally, private failure should be dealt with by private confrontation, confession and repentance. However, when failure becomes a public scandal, then the issue must be addressed in that domain. For instance, a church member has a 'one-off' moral lapse: she spent the night with her boyfriend and is now deeply repentant. On the other, a church elder leaves his wife and three young children for his secretary. Shame on the local church who cannot differentiate between the two situations and insists, for instance, on public confession by the young woman whilst saying nothing about the elder save that he has 'a few domestic problems.'

The principle of fellow leaders helping fallen leaders is well illustrated here. 'Ordinary church members' (a dreadful phrase, I admit) are sometimes not in possession of all the facts and must act very carefully towards a leader they suspect has a problem (see 1 Timothy 5:19 – I wish some church members remembered that verse when they are tempted to adopt a 'shoot to kill' policy towards their pastor). Paul has the facts, is not intimidated by Peter's reputation and is determined to stay loyal to the gospel. He knows that neither Peter nor himself is infallible. Scripture never holds before us plaster saints, perfect people: all leaders are flawed, save One. The gospel preaches One 'who had no sin' (2 Cor. 5:21), who, unlike the rest of us, does not have feet of clay but feet so strong that they can be described 'like bronze glowing in a furnace' (Rev. 1:15). And it is Jesus who precisely is the hope of every fallen sinner and saint (v14).

● *How easy is it for a church to gloss over leadership failings? What are some of the things that could happen as a result of such an attitude?*
● *What is the best way forward for an ordinary church member who suspects trouble at the top – especially when they are not in full possession of all the facts?*

IN PRINCIPLE ALL LEADERS ARE, LIKE ALL CHRISTIANS, RECOVERABLE

There's a dual goal to be achieved by Paul's actions here: the first is the safeguarding of 'the truth of the gospel', the second is the restoration of Peter to get him back 'in line with the truth' (v14). The logic of Paul's words here, not to say almost their humour, is irresistible. If religion of any kind can be compared to a drug, then Peter is like an addict set free after years of bondage and now trying to 'force' (v14) his family and friends to 'get hooked', suggesting that such addiction may somehow help them eventually to be drug free. Ridiculous!

When any Christian falls into serious sin, it seems to me that there are three possibilities. The most drastic is that the Lord 'takes them home early to heaven', as someone has put it (1 Cor. 11:30; 1 Jn. 5:16). The second is they languish on the side of the track, 'disqualified for the prize' (1 Cor. 9:27) not of salvation but for services rendered – a life of just 'wood, hay or straw' (1 Cor. 3:12). The third option is the Lord's gracious recovery of the offender. Someone heeds the rebuke, swallows their pride, takes the medicine and makes a great recovery.

And Peter? We already know him as a big man who had been restored once before (Jn. 18:27; 21:15-19). What would he do now? Dig in, fight his corner or take Paul's rebuke on the chin? If we turn to the Council of Jerusalem (Acts 15), this very issue of whether Gentiles were to live like Jews was central. Yet in a compelling speech, Peter argued that it was wrong to burden the Gentiles with a yoke even Jews could not carry. 'No!' he said, 'we believe it is through the grace of our Lord Jesus that we are saved, just as they are' (Acts 15:11). In essence, he was saying that Paul was right, he was wrong: we are not saved by our law-keeping but 'through the grace of our Lord Jesus', Paul's argument all the way through Galatians.

Perhaps the reader of these paragraphs has been badly let down by a fellow Christian, a friend, a parent, a minister. Maybe you are massively confused, still hurting and mad at God, especially as the person in question never seemed to get what's coming to them. I have no excuses for another's behaviour in the name of Christ that has deeply wounded you. But may I venture two questions? First, have you got 'What's coming to you'? The grace of the Lord Jesus is the only thing that prevents any of us getting what *we* deserve. Second, is it possible that the offender has done more than you think to put things right and that a changed life is saying so? It may not be, of course. But if the answer is positive, then you need to cut that person a bit of slack and find help to move on mentally and spiritually yourself. Maybe you are that leader who has done something despicable. Is recovery possible?

● *Stop and reflect on the questions in the last paragraph, if appropriate.*

Some years ago, at about one in the morning, I was sitting on the hard shoulder of the M1 motorway, with home still over one hundred miles away. My car engine had blown up for a second time in ten weeks. Eventually a truck with a trailer appeared. I showed my little card to the driver: RAC Rescue & Recovery Service. The car was duly hoisted onto the trailer. At 4.00 am, the vehicle was pushed off the trailer and parked outside my home. I quipped, 'It's one way to save petrol, right?' The RAC man never even smirked!

God is in the 'Rescue and Recovery' business. In Jesus Christ he has come to save the world, Jews and Gentiles alike. The grace of God introduces me to the God of grace who rescued and restored Peter. Do you know what grace may do for us? Just the same. And when the Lord recovers his own, he's never straight-faced but will 'rejoice over you with singing' (Zeph. 3:17). If that doesn't bring a smile to our faces, what will?

FURTHER STUDY

In the story of David and Bathsheba (2 Sam. 11,12) we can see the anointed king, a man after God's own heart, committing the most heinous act. David sleeps with another man's wife; she becomes pregnant, and when his attempts at deception don't work, he arranges the man's death. Once his sin was pointed out to him, David was truly sorry (Ps. 51). He was restored to God, but his wrongdoing had tragic consequences.

REFLECTION AND RESPONSE

- It's sad when any Christian sins, not least because their witness to Christ is compromised or even ruined. But when a leader sins, it can have far-reaching effects. How can we help our leaders stand firm against temptation?

- Think about the importance of accountability. Are your church leaders accountable to anyone? Commit to praying regularly for one of your leaders. Ask them if there are any particular issues they would like you to pray about.

- If you are a leader, think about who you are accountable to. If you know you have an area of particular weakness, are you willing to share this with an accountability partner?

SMALL GROUP DISCUSSION POINT
Talk about ways you could encourage your leadership, especially those who are pastors and teachers in the church.

CHAPTER 6

I did it my way

GALATIANS 2:15-21

Aim: To consider what it really means to be justified by faith

> **FOCUS ON THE THEME:**
> To 'justify' means to declare righteous in the sight of God. Spend a few minutes praising him that this is how he sees you right now . . . justified in his sight! Begin this session by singing a chorus or hymn, or playing a CD track which focuses on justification by faith (for example, Stuart Townend and Keith Getty's *In Christ Alone*).

Reading: Galatians 2:15-21
Key verse: Galatians 2:16b

There are millions of people in Great Britain today who 'lead lives of quiet desperation', as Henry David Thoreau once put it. You only need to take a trip on the London underground in any rush hour to see what I mean. Faces that are exhausted, simply highlighting people living on the edge; emotionally, physically and psychologically fatigued. And it's possible that religion can contribute to that sad state of affairs.

Religious faith can easily add a dimension of pressure that turns up the temperature in the pressure cooker of life. One of the reasons, I think, why many people in the western world have abandoned traditional Christianity and sometimes turned to eastern faiths and alternative spiritualities is that these can appear to offer remedies for coping with life's pressures. They seem to promise a path to personal wholeness, harmony and inner peace. In contrast, Christian faith can be presented as the religion of the constant 'do' – welcome to the church of perpetual obligation. How come? I believe it is to do with the kind of issues that Paul addresses in this section of the letter. If we misunderstand at this point, then we have a form of Christianity that is summed up by the phrase 'the law', used six times in this section. In essence, the law's demands can be summarised in one word, 'Do!' It is possible to profess our belief in 'the grace of God' (v21), yet in our experience to behave like it's all down to us. No-one can avoid pressure – in our homes, families, workplaces and churches. But law without grace can drive us to the very edge of despair. Is there hope?

Before we answer that question, I need to enter a caveat about these verses and on into chapter 3. They are the most difficult to grapple with in the whole of the letter, and have produced a mass of scholarly reflection in the last few years alone. Scholars like N.T. Wright[2] have suggested new approaches as to how best to read these verses. Other scholars, such as Mark Seifrid and Philip Eveson, have heavily criticised what is known as this 'New Perspective' on Paul.[3] You may wish to follow some of this up in more detail – see endnotes.

What is clear is that Paul is writing in the white heat of theological confusion, and is answering objections and questions that his opponents had raised. That said, the main contours are clear as he outlines the relationship between justification and faith (vs 15-16), justification and works (vs 17-18), and justification and new life (vs 19-21). The relevance of what is here, for this or any other century, should become abundantly clear. So, to repeat, is there hope? Yes, of course there is hope: resources are available for the guilt-ridden, the jaded and the totally lost and confused.

JUSTIFICATION AND FAITH (15,16)

Two ministers, one very strict, the other a little more relaxed, lived in the same town. The latter approached the former with a view to some joint efforts for the gospel. The strict minister did not see how they could, his ministerial colleague not being as 'sound' as he. In sheer exasperation the more relaxed responded, 'But, brother, we are both trying to do the Lord's work.' 'Aye,' came the reply, 'you in your way and I in his!' In these verses we are face to face with doing it 'My way' or 'his' when it comes to Christian faith and living. The argument here becomes more directly doctrinal than the biographical ones that have preceded it. In addition, we are not sure where the quote marks should start or finish: did Paul say all of this (vs 15-21) to Peter or does his public rebuke finish at the end of verse 14? Either way, we are invited to listen in.

Centuries before Christ, one of Job's friends asked a most pertinent question that religion seeks to answer: 'How then can a man be righteous before God? How can one born of woman be pure?' (Job 25:4). Note the phrase 'righteous before God', not simply before others. How indeed, when according to the Bible none of us in God's sight is 'full of natural goodness', as a milk advert years ago suggested we would be if we drank the stuff? Of course, we have not all committed the same sins; we are not all equally outrageous. But we all belong to the same broken and rebellious human race, 'fallen short of the glory of God' and heading for 'death' (Rom. 3:23, 6:23). On the night of 14/15 April 1912 the Titanic sank. Stowaways and millionaires, cabin crew and the captain were all on the same sinking ship. Before God, we too are all in the same boat. In these verses, we are reminded of God's rescue package, his way of salvation.

For the first time in Galatians, Paul uses the word justification. What does it mean? It is a legal term, drawn from the courts. Two men are there, the plaintiff and the defendant. What is required of the judge, having reviewed the evidence? The book of Deuteronomy tells us: 'When men have a dispute, they are to take it to court and the judges will decide the case, acquitting the innocent and condemning the guilty' (Deut. 25:1). Of course, there can be corruption in human courts: 'Acquitting the guilty and condemning innocent – the Lord detests them both' (Prov. 17:15). But when the system is just, the judge makes a declaration to the effect that the person is not guilty, or is 'in the right', and therefore free before the eyes of the law in the terms of the case before it. To be 'justified' is the opposite of being 'condemned.' Justification does not *make* someone righteous. If I am before the courts for a traffic offence, but the evidence shows the speed camera lied (warning: it usually doesn't), I walk free from the charges before the court. Am I now a paragon of virtue in every other sphere of my life? Hardly. But with reference to this particular offence I am in the right, I am justified. The question is, how can that happen *before* God, how does such justification come about?

Three times here Paul uses the phrase 'observing the law' (v16), literally 'by works of law.' This is God's law, of course, not only the Ten Commandments but all the others too. The rabbis reckoned there were 613 of them: 365 'Don'ts' (one for each day of the year!) and 248 'Dos.' In the context, however, the Judaisers probably emphasised circumcision, Sabbath observance and *kosher* food laws, the three 'big badges' that said you were Jewish. So keep these laws especially, and you are well and truly in with God. Really? Paul replies: 'a man is not justified by observing the law . . . because by observing the law no one will be justified' (lit. 'all flesh'– no exceptions). That is not the way to peace with God. Indeed, rather than showing a holy life-style, 'keeping the rules' may degenerate into merely showing off, boasting, but not in the cross of Christ (6:14). Of course, not all first century Jews were into 'merit theology': check out the godly folk in the first two chapters of Luke's gospel, for instance. But in Galatia, Paul's opponents were in danger of such a theology, when they ought to have known that 'we who are Jews by birth . . . know that a man is not justified by observing the law' (v15f). Concern for the law can easily slip into legalism.

Today, 'legalism' is sometimes bandied around by some Christians as a slur on other Christians who are perhaps more strict than they are over certain issues (alcohol, styles of worship, forms of dress etc). Most times I have heard the accusation it has been used inaccurately. True legalism is this: the belief that by my doing 'my part' and God doing his, then one day I will be justified. The equation works like this:

Faith in Christ + my good works
= the fruit of justification on the last day

Indeed, if one talks to many people about their need of Christ, very often they will tell you that they are basically a good person, though they may not believe in God or go to church. Push them further and you will find that some kind of merit theology is at work in their hearts: 'I've always done my best, been kind, never done anybody any harm, tried to behave myself.' The implication is that if they do stand before God one day and give an account of themselves, on balance their good will outweigh their bad and, if there is a heaven, they have accumulated enough air miles to get there.

In contrast, three times this verse tells us, in slightly different phrases, that is by 'faith in Jesus Christ' that we are made right with God. The Bible's equation is radically different:

Faith in Christ
= justification now, works being the fruit of justification

But what does 'faith in Christ' (lit. 'the faith of Christ) mean? The generally accepted way to understand the phrase, paralleled by 'believing what you heard' (3:2), is for it to mean that I place *my* faith in and commit *myself* to Christ. It is the believer's trust in Jesus. However, more recently, a number of scholars have suggested, since faith can also mean faithfulness, that it is 'the faith and the faithfulness of Jesus.' In other words, it refers to the Lord Jesus' own faith in God and his perfect obedience to his Father and his law: Jesus lived the life we ought to have lived and, acting as our representative, he died and rose again. Therefore he is the objective ground for faith. Perhaps both shades of meaning are here, since our response should be to 'put our faith in Christ Jesus', i.e. we trust in the faithful One himself.

Either way, it is vital that we do not make 'faith' a 'work.' We are not saved *on account of* our faith, but on account of Jesus. But how do I access the benefits of Jesus, how am I justified? Is it through my works, what I can *do*, or through faith in what Christ has *done*? If it is works, then I can never know I have done enough. But if I am relying on Christ, I am trusting One who has done everything necessary to bring me home to God for time and forever:

Upon a life I did not live,
Upon a death I did not die,
Another's life, Another's death,
I rest my whole eternity.

It is not in *what* we have faith but in *whom*.

● *After salvation we so much want to 'work for God' but he*
  says, 'I don't want you to work for me. I want to do my work
  in and through you!' How does this work?

JUSTIFICATION AND WORKS (17,18)

The previous section's insistence that we are justified by
faith, or 'by grace you have been saved, through faith . . .
not by works,' (Eph. 2:8-9), has often been dismissed along
these lines: this is all a legal fiction and morally quite
dangerous. If you tell people that already, in the here and
now and on into the future, there is 'no condemnation for
those who are in Christ Jesus' ('condemnation' being the
opposite of justification, Romans 8:1), they may well retort,
'Are we to continue in sin that grace may abound?' (Rom.
6:1 RSV). Although there are other approaches to
interpreting verses 17 and 18, it seems to me that the
Judaisers were arguing along such lines. I suspect it went
something like this.

'Paul, your idea of Gentile justification and therefore
inclusion amongst the people of God on the basis of faith in
Christ alone is highly dangerous. True, they may get in
initially by faith, but they need standards now to live by
and the law of Moses alone provides them.' In other words,
people may profess to believe in Christ and yet live anyway
they like: 'it becomes evident that we ourselves are sinners
. . . [and therefore] Christ promotes sin' (v17). Inevitably,
that raises the thorny question of the relationship between
faith and works, between being 'declared right' and 'living
righteously.' Church history abundantly illustrates the
tension. Sometimes, the Church has so insisted on 'works'
that it appeared that one could buy salvation, as happened
notoriously with the sale of indulgences in the sixteenth
century, a way of reducing a loved one's period in

purgatory. The revulsion felt by Martin Luther and others at such teaching helped spark the Protestant Reformation. Other times, notorious characters have appeared, proclaiming that the more one sins the more there is to forgive, so more grace is needed and in exercising it God is more glorified.

Back to the courtroom. If the gospel simply teaches that God, the Judge, lets us off, no matter what we do, so long as we have believed in Jesus, and he is not at all bothered about our present or future behaviour, then the cry of 'Outrageous' would be correct. I am sitting here typing away on the day I heard a news item that a paedophile was released on police bail, and during that period of freedom, whilst awaiting further investigation, committed a further offence against an eleven-year old child. Shocking, dreadful. But the truth of the gospel is that when God justifies us we are 'justified *in Christ*' (v17), a phrase Paul uses dozens of times in his letters. Why? Because justification does not happen in isolation. It is part of a whole salvation package that includes reconciliation to God, adoption into his family and the work of his Spirit in our hearts and lives to transform us (4:6). Indeed, one day we will be like Christ (1 Jn. 3:2), and 'conformed to the likeness of his Son . . . glorified', to use Paul's language (Rom. 8:29f). The Judge who acquits me now takes me on as one of his children, adopting me into his family, and infusing his Holy Spirit into my heart so that faith begins to express 'itself through love' (5:6). And he can do this absolutely justly because Jesus, the Son of God, has paid our penalty and died our death (vs19-21).

The foregoing helps to answer Paul's question, 'does . . . Christ promote sin?' and his passionate retort, 'Absolutely not!' ('God forbid' AV). If someone professes faith yet continues to live a godless life, what the gospel sought to 'destroy' – sin – is rebuilt and the person's life is saying 'I am a law-breaker' (v18). Do you recall the story of the woman taken in the very act of adultery in John 8? Jesus says two things to her: 'neither do I condemn you' and 'leave your life of sin' (Jn. 8:11). The gospel proclaims simultaneously 'No condemnation' and a call to a transformed life through Christ who 'lives in me' (v20). Faith and repentance, belief and subsequent behaviour, justification and transformation are not enemies but friends. Christian lives become distorted when these complementary truths are driven apart. Does that mean Christians are here and now perfect? Don't they still sin? Yes, they do (see 1 John 1:7-10 for a reality check for those who think they don't). How we need verses 19-21!

● *How would you explain the relationship between being declared right and living righteously to someone who believes 'Oh, you Christians are all right. You can do what you like and get forgiven for it, can't you?'*

JUSTIFICATION AND NEW LIFE (19-21)

When our children were small, we were out one day walking in the Forest of Dean. Soon we were confronted by a massive tree, seemingly reaching up to the heavens, very wonderfully alive. But there was a problem: a huge chunk of it had been almost totally severed from the main trunk, and it lay there broken, scattered all over the path and its surrounding area. The broken off chunk, just barely attached, was quite lifeless. In these verses, Paul addresses issues of death and life. He talks about his having 'died to the law, so that I might live for God' (v19), being 'crucified with Christ' but Christ living in him (v20). Somehow he is both dead and yet wonderfully alive, just like that tree in the forest. How can this be?

'For through the law I died to the law so that I might live for God.' The law of God has a penalty for transgression – condemnation and death. I must face that penalty either personally and I die, or I may face it representatively, if someone were to take my place. Here's 'the Son of God' (v20), whose 'faith and faithfulness' made him the perfect human being. When he came before the bar of God's law, all heaven declared, 'Justified!' There were no charges to answer because he was guiltless. The Bible is emphatic on this point (Is. 53:9; Mt. 27:19; Lk. 23:41,47; 2 Cor. 5:21; Heb. 7:26; 1 Pet. 2:22; 1 Jn. 3:5). Yet he was crucified, suffering a felon's death (3:13). Here we are at the heart of what is called the Bible's atonement theology, how we get 'at-one-ment' with God. Some background is necessary if we are to understand Paul here.

The word 'Christ' is the Greek equivalent of the Jewish 'Messiah', the long-promised One who would undo ultimately all the evil in the world, stretching right back to the dawn of the human race and its forefather, Adam. When Adam disobeyed God (Gen. 3), he plunged the whole human race into sin and darkness, and the very physical world around him was likewise affected. Paul tells us that 'sin entered the world through' that first Adam (Rom. 5:12). Now a 'last Adam' (1 Cor. 15:45) has come, and through his life, death and resurrection has set in process a chain of events that will ultimately lead to his return in glory and his 'making everything new' (Rev. 21:5). When a person is connected by faith to this Adam, Jesus, what is true of him becomes true of them: they have 'died', 'have been crucified' in the Messiah, his death counting for them. In him they rise to a new life. By birth, every person entering this world is in the first Adam. By new birth, any person can come into the Last Adam, the new humanity, Christ. How can this happen?

It is through the 'Son of God' who 'loved me and gave himself for me' says Paul. The result is that life 'in the body' can now be lived for Jesus, the One who 'lives in me' (v20). Paul's opponents' objections to his gospel were along the lines of what is technically called 'antinomianism' – 'Paul, if what you assert is believed, people will live how they like, breaking God's law.' Paul will have none of it. 'Don't you understand?' we can almost hear him say, 'I have a whole different motivation now to live a God-pleasing life.' 'Rightness' with God and the righteous life that is meant to flow from it cannot be 'gained through the law' and self-effort. If they could, then the death of Jesus was totally in vain – 'Christ died for nothing!' Then 'the grace of God' is set aside (v21). However, when the truth of God's love in Christ hits our spiritual psyche, we exclaim with Isaac Watts

> Love so amazing, so divine
> Demands my soul, my life, my all.

What I am describing here, being made like Christ, living for Jesus, is called 'sanctification', or has sometimes been known as 'the doctrine of gratitude.' How does it work? There is just two years between my younger sister and me, so we did a lot of our growing up together. In her teens, there was always conflict when she had to perform any domestic duty. However, one day, while a pal and I were sitting there, just minding our own business, she suddenly appeared like a tornado, and everything was being cleaned – ourselves included if we did not move! Why the change? A new boyfriend was coming home. She was 'in love' (again!) One day she was lethargic, now she was possessed of a new energy. What she wouldn't do 'under law', she did gladly 'under grace', the motivation that flowed through a new relationship called love.

A young medical student once read a tract entitled *The Finished Work of Christ*. Through it, he committed his life to Christ. He went on to be an outstanding missionary pioneer to China. His name was Hudson Taylor. The effect of its message he later recorded: 'I saw that the whole work was done. The whole debt was paid. There was nothing more for me to do but to accept what he offered and praise him ever more.' That's gratitude for you.

● *Love motivates us to act in a way that obligation cannot. How far is love a motivation in your Christian life? Have some things become 'a duty' whereas they were once carried out through sheer love and gratitude to God?*

FURTHER STUDY
In Ephesians 2:1-10 we read that we are seated with Christ in the heavenly realms; this is our spiritual position. Seated implies not working . . . relaxing . . . resting in Christ's finished work.

REFLECTION AND RESPONSE
- Spend some time reflecting on the fact that Jesus' sacrifice was sufficient for your salvation. Like a drowning person, we must resist all attempts to save ourselves. We must let go and let our Rescuer do it all.

- The big question is, 'Are you doing it *his* way, or are you doing it *your* way?' In your attitude to Christian living, are you more like the lost son – or the lost son's older brother (Lk. 15:11-31)? How far do you feel you are still 'working' as a Christian, and frankly not enjoying it, where Christ may be asking you to rest in him? Write down anything that comes to mind, and read what you have written through before the Lord. If you have written down any areas where you know you should be resting in his finished work, but are doing things your way, ask his forgiveness and then rip up the paper.

- Make a list of all the things you are grateful to God for. Can you include difficult areas of your life?

SMALL GROUP DISCUSSION POINT
Think about what you have learned here about doing it his way as
opposed to your way. Do we as Christians demand more of each
other than God does? What effect can this have on us as individuals
and as a fellowship? Discuss.

CHAPTER 7

Bewitched, bothered and bewildered

GALATIANS 3:1-5

Aim: To be challenged by what it means to begin with – and stay in – the Spirit

FOCUS ON THE THEME:
Imagine you are with a friend, waiting for a bus. Your friend has two heavy shopping bags and feels very burdened by the load. Thankfully, the bus soon arrives. Oh dear! Standing room only! Then you see that your friend has not put the bags down – she still has a tight hold of them. You suggest she puts them on the floor and lets the bus take the strain, and her face brightens. What a relief. What things in your life have been a huge relief?

Reading: Galatians 3:1-5
Key verse: Galatians 3:5

There's a huge welfare scandal going on in Great Britain. People who are rightfully entitled to huge benefits are being swindled out of them. Resources are available, the costs are all covered, yet these folk live in poverty, and this time it is not the government's fault. I reckon there are tens of thousands of Christian believers living as if Pentecost never happened, as if the Spirit of God had never come. They subsist on or below the spiritual poverty line because they fail to realise that God has generously donated through Jesus the wondrous gift of his Holy Spirit, to deliver us from mediocre Christianity and to enable us to live life to the full in Christ.

Nowadays, the very mention of the Spirit can be so controversial. If, some forty years ago, the Holy Spirit was the forgotten member of the Trinity, today he is often the most misunderstood member. We divide churches along party lines of whether we are charismatic, non-charismatic, anti-charismatic, etc. Whatever our label, I sometimes fear that many of us are being cheated out of heaven's desire for us to live in all the benefits of Christ, knowing we are loved by God, accepted and forgiven, and indwelt by the Spirit of the living God.

Similarly, it was some form of 'benefits fraud' that these Galatian believers were facing. False teachers threatened their welfare in Christ. Recently, while three UK government cabinet ministers were facing personal challenges to their respective offices, *The Daily Telegraph* summed up their plight with the telling headline 'Bewitched, bothered, bewildered.' It could have been written for these believers: 'Who has bewitched you?' asks Paul indignantly. False teachers had, and were threatening to rob them of their privileges in Christ, swindling them out of his benefits and leaving them confused and adrift from the wondrous grace of God provided by the Holy Spirit, who is mentioned three times in these verses.

This section could be usefully subtitled Question Time, as six questions are fired off in a rapid salvo. Why? The purpose is to encourage us to do the one thing so many Christians seem loath to do when they are in trouble: think. 'You foolish Galatians!' picks up a word used by Jesus to the two on the Emmaus Road when they likewise were 'foolish and slow of heart' (Lk. 24:25) to believe the truth. 'You dear idiots of Galatia!' is how J.B. Phillips' translation has it. They were allowing these false teachers to bemuse them. So, as a wise pastor, Paul starts with them where they are in terms of their own experience of being Christians, before dealing directly with Scripture (6-9).

Six question marks appear in our text, but as the beginning of verse 3 is the question form of 'You foolish Galatians' (v1), we will reduce them to five.

A QUESTION OF DECEPTION

'Who has bewitched you?' Bewitched is a strong word, drawn from the realm of sorcery, and used of 'putting an evil eye' on somebody to hoodwink them. Paul may, of course, be using the word metaphorically. The false teachers were 'spellbinding' in their teaching and approach. However, we do well to remember that behind all false teaching is the one who bears the title of 'the father of lies', according to Jesus (Jn. 8:44). Heresy is just as damnable in Scripture as adultery, and we must not be indifferent to false teaching as if it doesn't matter. It matters a great deal. This brand of Jewish Christianity suggested that the Lord Jesus was not quite good enough but that 'righteousness could be gained through the law' (2:21). But this isn't 'the truth of the gospel' (2:14). What is? 'Before your very eyes Jesus Christ was clearly portrayed as crucified' (v1) recalling perhaps the very graphic way Paul preached the cross of Christ as central to the gospel of redeeming love. Indeed, the tense of the Greek verb 'crucified' is important: it implies that Christ was not only crucified historically, but that the results of that are as present and powerful today. Christ had not 'died for nothing' (2:21), but had paid the full price of salvation.

With that in mind, we do well to remind ourselves that the gospel is not, in the first instance, an invitation for us to do something. It is a declaration of what God has done. It declares, 'Look! Christ has died in pain and shame and agony to bring a rebel race back to God!' And we are then commanded to believe it, trust Christ, turn to and follow him as the only reasonable step imaginable. When that happens, all the benefits of the work of Christ become ours by the Spirit. But how does that happen? On to Paul's second question.

A QUESTION OF RECEPTION

A key question in many churches today is how do we receive the Holy Spirit? Does the experience just happen, is it a second experience, is it for the few? Paul's question is highly pertinent: 'Did you receive the Spirit by observing the law, or by believing what you heard?' The answer?

It was obvious, really. Here were Gentiles, people who didn't follow *kosher* food laws, keep the Sabbath and other festivals or practise circumcision. Some may have been God fearers but many were pagans. Yet they heard and saw Christ 'clearly portrayed as crucified' (v1), believed what they heard and thus received God's gift of the Holy Spirit (v2). Do you see that? When they embraced the gospel, the Spirit of God embraced them. Do you notice how closely the Lord Jesus and his Spirit are tied together here?

I recall hearing an evangelist say, 'As I am preaching to you tonight, I am praying that you will be hearing Another voice, beyond mine, speaking to you.' In some wonderful way, as the gospel of the crucified Lord is proclaimed, Another is at work, as mysteriously and silently as the wind (Jn. 3:8), wooing, convincing and eliciting faith and repentance in Christ among the hearers. Later in chapter 3, Paul will once again draw these strands together: Christ 'redeemed us in order that the blessing given to Abraham might come to the Gentiles through Christ Jesus' (3:14). What was the blessing given to Abraham? Part of it was that 'The Scripture foresaw that God would justify the Gentiles by faith' (3:8), one side of the coin of salvation being justification. The other side is the reality, 'that by faith we might receive the promise of the Spirit' (3:14). The initial part of becoming a Christian is that I am justified; God says 'You're right with me.' That's objective, non-experiential. But at the same moment, the Spirit of God takes up residence in my heart, and begins a process of change in me. That is subjective and experiential. Elsewhere, Paul gives us his bottom line: 'if anyone does not have the Spirit of Christ, he does not belong to Christ' (Rom. 8:9). No-one is a Christian without believing the gospel; no-one can be a believer and be without the Holy Spirit. The DNA of every Christian, the 'genetic fingerprint' that marks them off as children of God, is to believe the gospel and receive the Spirit. That's foundational.

In the experience of local church life, however, we often seem to enjoy our polarities. In some churches, it would be permissible to ask, although everything seems orthodox, 'Did you receive the Spirit?' In others, although the atmosphere is one of a spiritual 'rave', the question would be, is Christ regularly 'portrayed as crucified' (v1) here? But what the Bible has joined together, the gospel and the Holy Spirit, no-one should separate.

And what about personal experience? The well-known C.H. Spurgeon put it well: 'I looked to Christ and the dove of peace flew to my heart; I looked to the dove and he flew away.' If the Spirit's ministry is to glorify the Lord Jesus (Jn. 16:14), and it is the Lord Jesus who is the donor of the Spirit (Acts 2:33), then it is to him I look and through him I receive the Spirit of God. In that sense, I am complete, just like a newborn babe. All that is required is that I grow, to 'live by the Spirit'. . . to 'keep in step with the Spirit' (5:25), and see to it that 'the fruit of the Spirit' is being reproduced in me (5:22). In other words, I need to keep going and growing.

● *How do you see the Holy Spirit working in your life and in your church?*

This leads us to Paul's next question.

A QUESTION OF COMPLETION

Paul once again draws a contrast, this time between the Spirit and 'human effort' (v3), literally 'the flesh', that is unaided human activity, devoid of the Spirit of God. Is the flesh the way to 'perfection', one of the ways of translating 'attain your goal' (v3)? It seems that the Judaisers were suggesting something along the lines that grace may get you in, but works of the law will keep you in. Phillips' translation captures the polemical, almost sarcastic tone of the question: 'Surely you can't be so idiotic as to think that a man begins his spiritual life in the Spirit and then completes it by reverting to outward observances?' They knew from experience that, when they trusted Christ, the Spirit of God came and they received new life. How could they now conclude that new life could be sustained by outward observances?

Evangelical churches are not immune from such temptations. On the one side, there are some who are very traditional, always seeming to invoke the 'eleventh commandment' – 'Thou shalt not': you must not do that, you can't go there, you dare not go near that other group of believers. *Externalism* becomes a real temptation: we know how spiritual someone is by their outward attendance at church etc. On the other side, there are those who profess to be truly free, 'not under law', so they only read their Bibles or attend church when they are so led. They are certainly not relying on outward observances: rather, it is inner ones that are all important – hunches, leadings, intuitions, 'my heart tells me' type of stuff. They are in real danger of a *mysticism* that may carry them away from Jesus and his gospel. The truth lies beyond both these admitted caricatures of some Christians.

We can think of the problem along the lines of an analogy. At one level, the law of God demands that I fly. The difficulty is, it cannot provide me with wings. But the gospel does. It invites me to step on board the Jumbo jet of grace, what God has done in Jesus, and promises to fly me, for purposes of this illustration, over an Atlantic Ocean that starts here and ends with eternity. Imagine being on a plane halfway across the Atlantic, and someone on board suggesting to you that there is another way, a 'higher, better way', of completing the trip. You are to jump from the plane, without a parachute, hit the water and then swim the other 1500+ miles under your own steam! I remember an old Marx Brothers' film in which the three brothers had stowed away on a ship across the Atlantic. When it docked in America their problem of disembarking without being caught was answered by their discovering some Russian generals' uniforms. Suitably clad, they were greeted by a press conference about why they had chosen to come to America by sea and not by air. Groucho, the usual spokesman, tells the press that they had tried to fly, but the first time, half way across the Atlantic, the plane began to run out of fuel, so they had to return to Europe. The second time, they got three-quarters of the way, only for the same thing to reoccur, and once more they flew back to Europe. Great farce! Great entertainment! Ridiculous! But no more so than anyone who thinks to make it from here to eternity without Christ and his empowering Spirit *all the way*. Of

course, the Judaisers did not like that truth, and they
exerted pressure on these young converts that spilled over
into potential violence.

● *How can we hold onto the fact that throughout our*
  Christian lives, it is Christ who sustains us?

A QUESTION OF PERSECUTION

Most religions teach both a love for God and for one's
neighbour. However, religions have their truth claims;
Judaism, Christianity and Islam included. To have a faith
worth dying for is one thing. To have one worth killing for
is quite another. Paul himself, before his conversion, has
already reminded us of that type of religion (1:13). Some of
the Jewish Christians, though not prepared to go that far, of
course, nevertheless were more than happy to bring all
sorts of pressure to bear on these Galatian believers: 'Have
you suffered so much for nothing?' Paul asks. 'Suffered'
here, from which we get words like 'pathology', could be
translated in a more positive sense, 'to experience.' So the
New English Bible translates it as, 'Have all your great
experiences been in vain?' However, the overall context of
the epistle suggests that the idea of suffering is the correct
one. For instance, Paul later says that, 'Those who want to
make a good impression outwardly are trying to compel
you to be circumcised. The only reason they do this is to
avoid being persecuted for the cross of Christ' (6:12). That
verse in turn sheds light on why these Judaisers were
overbearing: they themselves were probably in danger of
persecution from some zealous, unconverted 'Pauls' of first
century Judaism too.

Suffering for the gospel to the point of physical violence
and death is not a familiar, firsthand experience for many

western based Christians today. But it is for many believers in other parts of the world. I recall with joy that morning over twenty years ago when I baptised a young Indian medical doctor, Kailash. He subsequently returned to his home in north India, set up a clinic, shared the love of Jesus with all he could and paid the ultimate price in being martyred for his efforts. In the West, however, generally speaking, the pressures are more subtle: keep your faith private in the workplace; don't try to convert anybody; don't take a stand on morality; be indifferent to the plight of the hungry; don't let your lifestyle or your spending suggest you are any different to your non-Christian neighbours.

In addition, we should not underestimate the 'hatchet job' the media often perform on Evangelical Christians, especially those 'flat earth' ones who have the audacity to believe that God, not blind, evolutionary forces, created the world. A recent Home Secretary had the temerity, in the wake of the bombings in London on 7 July 2005, to speak about Islamic terrorists and fundamentalist Christians as if they were both part of the same problem of extremism. I suspect, barring a revival of biblical faith, in the words of a Nat King Cole song, 'there may be trouble ahead' for faithful Christians living in western Europe. After all, our Master warned us that in 'this world you will have trouble' (Jn. 16:33), and Paul added that 'everyone who wants to live a godly life in Christ Jesus will be persecuted' (2 Tim. 3:12). Why be a Christian then, is it 'really . . . for nothing' (v4)? Not at all. The final question reminds us of the privileges that are ours in Jesus.

● *We all have our personal preferences in worship and style of Christian living. But our own views can sometimes serve to inhibit the freedom others enjoy. Is there any area where you might be trying to limit the freedom someone else enjoys?*

A QUESTION OF PROVISION

The volume of each question in this section seems to increase gradually. How could they be so 'bewitched' (v1) when they had received the Spirit (v2) who had been the very 'beginning' (v3) of their spiritual lives and the source of their strength when they 'suffered so much' (v4)? Verse 5 then becomes something of a crescendo: 'Does God give you his Spirit and work miracles among you because you observe the law, or because you believe what you heard?' In this context, 'give' is a very strong word. It was the word used by someone who was footing the bill for providing a choir for a public event, for instance. Today, it may be compared to paying for a huge wedding reception for a daughter. One word sums it up: costly. To provide lavishly, you need to be very generous indeed. That is how God is: mightily generous, he is prepared to stand the bill and pay the cost of redeeming human beings through his Son and now donating his Spirit extravagantly to his people so that he even works 'miracles among' and/or 'in' them (v5).

'Miracles', now that's another touchy subject. As I have indicated in the previous paragraph, it is possible to translate miracles as happening either 'among' or 'in' them, and possibly both are included. At one level, every Christian should be a 'walking miracle', since what conversion does is to set up a whole new disposition in the human soul. Without Christ the human heart was a 'heart of stone'; now it is 'a new heart . . . a heart of flesh', because God promised, 'I will put my Spirit in you and move you to follow my decrees' (check out this great gospel prophecy in Ezekiel 36:26f). Here 'love, joy, peace' etc (5:22) may grow where once there was only hatred, misery and discord. In addition, pity the local church which no longer believes that her Lord can, or will, or does turn up and perform that which is truly inexplicable – a miracle – for his own sovereign purposes and glory and the good and benefit of his people. This is not a call to being gullible: too many 'faith healers' have given faith a bad name. But it is a reminder that we are dealing with a *living* God 'who treasures up his bright designs and works his sovereign will.'

● *Can you think of some answers to prayer that you have experienced? Thank God for his faith-building miracles.*

How does any of this happen? Is it because we keep the rules, 'observe the law', or because Christ keeps us as we believe what we have heard (v5)? The answer should be obvious.

A FINAL QUESTION

Since the Lord Jesus has ascended his heavenly throne, he's not physically present with us, nor is he spiritually absent. He still says: 'If any one loves me, he will obey my teaching. My Father will love him, and we will come to him and make our home with him' (Jn. 14:23). How? He comes to us by 'another Counsellor to be with you forever – the Spirit of truth' (Jn. 14:16-17). How is he received? By believing what we have heard (v5) in the gospel of Jesus, crucified, risen and reigning. And that living Jesus invites us to ask for more: 'If you then, though you are evil, know how to give good gifts to your children, how much more will your Father in heaven give the Holy Spirit to those who ask him' (Lk. 11:13).

Are we somewhat 'bewitched, bothered and bewildered', losing out on all the benefits that are ours in Christ? 'How much more?' is still the question. Day by day, we need to come to Christ and ask for his Spirit's power and grace to be at work in our churches, our homes and our hearts to work whatever miracles he wishes. The condition is that we 'ask him' or, more literally, 'keep on asking him.' Do we? That is a question I need to address every day.

FURTHER STUDY
Read Luke 24:49; Acts 1:4,8; 2:1-21. Praise God for the power that Jesus gives us so that we might live this new life in him.

REFLECTION AND RESPONSE
- 'As I am preaching to you tonight, I am praying that you will be hearing Another voice, beyond mine, speaking to you.' How open are you to the quiet voice of God's Spirit speaking into your life?

- Are you concerned about persecution when you share your faith, perhaps at work or even with your friends and family? Talk to God about your concerns now.

- Praise God that he still works miracles in our lives today – the new birth, the change in our lives, healing, deliverance.

SMALL GROUP DISCUSSION POINT
In Acts 12:1-17 we read the story of people gathered in prayer who received an answer they weren't expecting. Pray that you will know the boldness of the Holy Spirit, as the first believers did, to effectively share your faith. If anyone is struggling with a situation where they find it nearly impossible to do so, uphold them in prayer.

CHAPTER 8

Are you well connected?

GALATIANS 3:6-9

Aim: To examine the fact that our salvation is through the spiritual new birth alone

FOCUS ON THE THEME:
Someone once said, 'I work in a garage. It doesn't make me a car.' In the same way, going to church doesn't make us a Christian. What does?

Reading: Galatians 3:6-9
Key verse: Galatians 3:6

Some people are expert name droppers: 'When I was last speaking to the Prime Minister, he asked my advice about . . . '; 'Upon my most recent visit to Buckingham Palace, Her Majesty remarked that I should . . . ' and so on. If you are not that well connected, try your family tree: your genealogy is bound to contain aristocracy, even if it is twenty generations ago (and illegitimacy, imbecility and criminality too). It's all a game really, often played upon that great pitch called human pride. Sadly, it has its counterparts in church circles too: 'The Archbishop (of Canterbury, of course!) recently invited me to join. . .'; 'Dr Billy Graham said to me. . .'; 'During my daily phone call to Cliff Richard . . . '

Being well connected, having the right contacts and the correct ancestry, is part of the background to this chapter generally and this section in particular. It boils down to the question, 'Are you a child of Abraham?' and how that is decided; is it by birth or new birth?

One of the lines of spiritual seduction that the Judaisers were peddling ran something like this: the only people whom God favours are 'children of Abraham' (v7). How do you become a child of Abraham? That's straightforward – like Abraham, you must undergo circumcision (Gen. 17) and begin to keep the law of God. Then you will be right with God. In other words, you join us, you become Jewish essentially, and you are 'in' with God. Leaving aside the spiritual benefits or otherwise of that claim, the psychological boost must have been immensely attractive: you – once a poor, lost pagan – are now part of the great Jewish race, connected to the people of Abraham, a people with a history and a destiny. Lest we think this has no contemporary relevance, we ought to reflect on the fact that millions of people draw more than their spiritual security and strength from their conviction that they belong to the right religion, the true church or the correct religious organisation. They derive a sense of security and belonging from their particular group, and often a smugness in 'being right.' The Judaisers have many modern relatives.

As we shall presently see, Paul draws a different conclusion. But he can agree with the Judaisers that it is essential to have Abraham as one's spiritual father. The key issue is how that comes about. In the previous section (1-5), Paul has appealed to the Galatians' experience of the Spirit of God to address their 'bewitched, bothered and bewildered' state of mind. Now he will refer directly to Scripture. We may want to skim through Genesis 12-25 as the background music to what Paul says here. His tactic in taking these confused believers to the Bible is highly significant. For him and the early Christians, the Scriptures were the standard by which everything was to be judged. These days we talk about 'the canon' of Scripture, those 39 Old and 27 New Testament books that make up our Bible. And that word 'canon' is illuminating. Originally, it was a rule or straight edge, employed by a tailor or an architect, for instance. It gave you a standard by which to measure and judge things: was this piece of cloth the right length, was this wall straight?

The Galatians' experience was important, but it was also useless before the false teachers if it did not ultimately accord with Scripture. There are some Christians who want to drive a wedge between their experience of the Spirit and Scripture. Which is more important? In an ideal world, of course, the answer should be that they dovetail beautifully together. Helpfully, the ESV shows how closely tied this passage is to the previous section by translating 'by hearing with faith – just as Abraham "believed God."' But if there is an either/or choice, as there often is – my experience or the word of God – the Scriptures must win every time. Why? Because they are the 'canon', the straight edge against which everything, including my experience, must be judged.

So, how does Paul address the issue of being rightly related to Abraham? He does so by dealing with Abraham's faith, children and blessing.

- *Who do you think are some of the modern Judaisers?*
- *When and how could 'experience' become a very real problem? What danger might it lead into?*

ABRAHAM'S FAITH

'Consider Abraham' (v6), suggests Paul and proceeds to quote Genesis 15:6. Here was an old man, already over seventy-five years of age (Gen. 12:4), married to a wife getting on in years. He was deeply aware of having no natural heir (Gen. 15:3). But one starlit night God took him outside his tent and said, 'Abraham, start counting the stars.' The naked eye can see about eight thousand of them in a clear Near-Eastern sky. You can imagine as Abraham begins, 'One, two, three . . . Two thousand seven hundred and nineteen . . . ' Perhaps the Lord interrupted him: 'Abraham, can you really count those stars?' 'I think so: two thousand seven hundred and . . . and . . . Er . . . Er . . . One, two, three . . . ' You get the point: 'No, Lord, I can't.' And God said to him, 'I'm going to make your descendants like that – innumerable!' (Gen. 15:5). To a man who had no future – as far as he was concerned he and his wife weren't going to have any children – God promised, 'I'm going to give you a child and a whole race.' And Abraham's response was that he simply 'believed God' (v6) and in that moment was right with his Maker.

Why was this believing 'credited to him as righteousness' (v6)? Does 'faith' in anyone or anything substitute for 'works' – a 'so long as you believe in something' type of attitude? Hardly! Abraham 'believed God', the God who had spoken to him, revealed himself and who made promises. So faith here is taking God at his word, trusting what he says, relying upon what he promises. And that promise of a child, of 'seed' (v16) is inextricably bound up with Jesus. Really?

Some people are puzzled about how people before the coming of Jesus ever got right with God. Paul tells us here that God 'announced the gospel in advance to Abraham' (v8). Now that is worth pondering. Do you recall what the Lord Jesus said of Abraham? He 'rejoiced at the thought of seeing my day; he saw it and was glad' (Jn. 8:56). Elsewhere, we are told that Old Testament saints believed these promises of God for a Saviour 'and welcomed them from a distance' (Heb. 11:13). How were they converted before Jesus? How are people converted today? Let's think of Abraham for a moment. He could look at his body and say, 'Lord, I'm dead. But I believe your promise of acceptance and a new life.' We likewise come to God spiritually dead, with nothing to offer but our sin. But when we trust in the 'seed', to Jesus, whose cross has paid our debt, we find in him new life. Old Testament believers looked *forward* to the cross, we look *back* and both of us discover that we are credited with righteousness (v6), justified by faith in Christ (v8).

Naturally, those Old Testament saints did not have all the light that we have this side of the coming of Jesus. But they had enough to know about 'the sufferings of Christ and the glories that would follow' (1 Pet. 1:11). Such faith is 'saving faith', an absolute transfer of my trust from anyone or anything, myself included, to Another who is totally trustworthy. This kind of faith acts like an electrical switch, for through it flows the current of God's righteousness and salvation into human hearts. Which hearts? That leads us to the question of Abraham's children.

● *When we believe God, we are credited with righteousness.*
How does knowing you have the righteousness of Christ
himself help you see yourself today?

ABRAHAM'S CHILDREN

Deeply ingrained in the Jewish psyche was the conviction that they were Abraham's children and he their father (Jn. 8:33-39). Such conviction was a bulwark when facing invaders, whether Assyrian or Roman. The Jews were proud of their physical ancestry and therein lay the great temptation to rely on it as if it were an 'open sesame' to God's blessing, without accompanying faith and obedience. Nevertheless, the Jewish conviction was straightforward enough: to be a child of Abraham you had to be born

Jewish or become such via (male) circumcision. With respect therefore to these Galatian believers, the inference from the Judaisers was that they were not truly Abraham's children until they underwent circumcision.

Do you recall the days when we all used cassettes for tape recording? More than once I had the experience of taping a particular piece of music over a previously recorded soundtrack and then discovering upon playing it back that, for whatever technical reasons, the original recording had not been fully erased and continued to play in the background of the new one. Likewise, when Paul suggests considering Abraham and how he found righteousness credited to him, a dual track is being played, the one here before us and the original recording found in Genesis. Paul's opponents felt they could clearly hear how Abraham got right with God. He did what God said, 'Be circumcised' (Gen. 17:10). Paul says, in effect, you are not hearing the music correctly: you have got its timing all jumbled up. Their chronology was out. The quotation in verse 6 from Genesis 15 comes two whole chapters before Abraham was circumcised in Genesis 17. Significant? Massively so! Abraham, unlike Judaism, had no Temple, no priesthood, no circumcision and was following no dietary laws, yet he was right with God! Check out a fuller version of this argument in Romans 4:9-12.

The result of Paul's statement is this: 'Understand, then, that those who believe are children of Abraham' (v7). What is he driving at? Simply, that it is trusting Abraham's God that brings rightness with him, not our religious performances. Religion can be highly dangerous to the soul. Hence, John the Baptist warns the Jewish leaders of his day of their danger: 'do not think you can say to yourselves, "We have Abraham as our father." I tell you out of these stones God can raise up children for Abraham' (Mt. 3:9). Similarly, our Lord challenges those who were using the same mantra, 'Abraham is our father' as a cover for sin: 'If you were Abraham's children . . . then you would do the things Abraham did' (Jn. 8:39). One's physical descent is not the key to spiritual grace and blessing.

To put it straightforwardly, some people really do think that because they are part of a certain race, or belong to a particular religion or have been through some sacred ceremony or other, then God is almost morally bound to give them an entry pass into his kingdom. What really matters, however, is a spiritual new birth that comes about through the gospel of Christ that makes us right with God (v3). After all, it was to a very religious man, Nicodemus, 'Israel's teacher' – a 'Professor of Theology', we might say – that Jesus said 'You must be born again' (Jn. 3:10,7). Such spiritual kinship to Abraham has a purpose: that we may be 'blessed along with Abraham' (v9).

● *'I was born a Christian. My mother and father were Christians. I've been christened and confirmed.' How would you share the truth of the gospel with someone who said this to you?*

ABRAHAM'S BLESSING

Sometimes the way to get to a word's meaning is not only to look at its synonyms, words that say the same thing, but also its antonyms, words that say the opposite. In the Bible, the opposite of 'blessing' is 'curse.' In the following section, Paul will talk specifically about the curse brought on by the law (v10). But once again we are listening to some background music from the Genesis tape, this time long before Abraham. What is wrong with the world as we see it today? The Bible's answer is that it labours under a curse, something that goes right back to the time when rebellious people were told, 'Cursed is the ground *because of you*' (Gen. 3:17). How does God intend to right his world that is full of rebellious people and his material creation affected by their rebellion? The answer is that all nations would be blessed through Abraham (v9). For sure, that is a huge blessing! What does it consist of?

In essence, it is twofold. First, God has to deal with the barrier of our sinfulness and, secondly, he also needs to renew sinful, mortal people who live in a ruined world. Thankfully, our need both of forgiveness and new life are accomplished through 'the gospel' (v8). In terms of sinful people, he justifies not only Jews but also 'the Gentiles by faith' (v8). Justification is God's declaration that rebels, whether Jews or Gentiles, may go free because their penalty, death, has been paid at the cross of Jesus (see the section 2:15ff). The result is that through Abraham's 'seed . . . Christ' (v16), all nations can be blessed (v8). Here is the 'big story' of the whole Bible: God is going to have a people 'from every tribe and language and people and nation' (Rev. 5:9) who are his children. All around the globe today there are hundreds of millions of Christians because the promise of blessing the world through the gospel is being fulfilled. And the great commission still bids Christians everywhere to 'go and make disciples of *all nations*' (Mt. 28:19). A local church that does not have such a desire to seek the lost – an evangelistic pulse, a missionary heartbeat – has itself become lost. The Lord's main agenda in his world is to 'build my church' (Mt. 16:18).

CONCLUSION – ARE YOU WELL CONNECTED?

A while ago I bought a new hosepipe, the best that I could afford and Argos could provide. When I tried to water the garden I discovered it wasn't long enough, but a friend came to the rescue by giving me a piece from an old hose. But the two hoses needed joining together. A bit of improvisation on my part with a piece of metal and a couple of clips soon sorted it, until I turned the tap on. There was plenty of water everywhere, except at the end of the hose! Another trip, this time to B&Q for a proper hose connector. Sorted? Not quite. This hose connector needed to be attached to a nozzle connector for each piece of hose. Yet another trip. This was beginning to become expensive in time and money! But with one new hose pipe, one old hose pipe, one hose connector and two nozzle connectors fitting together beautifully, it was with relief I saw water at the correct end of the hose gushing out abundantly. And such things are a parable . . .

Do we want to be well connected to God? Then we need the blessing of Abraham, which has two 'nozzle connectors', justification and a new life: the word of the gospel in our minds and the work of the Spirit in our hearts. But there is a 'hose connector' that makes them fit together properly, expressed five times in these verses: 'he believed God . . . those who believe . . . by faith . . . those who have faith . . . the man of faith.' Faith is that absolute transfer of trust from myself to Christ and all he has done. Are you well connected? If you belong to Christ, thank God you are.

FURTHER STUDY
Read Romans 4:9-12 in some different Bible versions. Let the meaning really sink in to your spirit. If you have time, read through Genesis 12-25 to be blessed by Abraham's whole story.

REFLECTION AND RESPONSE
• Can you remember the day of your spiritual new birth, or was it a gradual process? Write it down. Ask God for an opportunity to share this with someone who doesn't know Christ this week.

• Think about your family tree from a spiritual perspective. Draw a tree putting in Abraham at the top, then Jesus, and then those who played a part, however small, in bringing you to faith. Thank God for each one.

SMALL GROUP DISCUSSION POINT
'Saving faith is the absolute transfer of trust from myself to Christ and all he has done.' Share how real this is for you today, and discuss what you have learned this session. Spend time in prayer for each other, especially if anyone is struggling to see themselves as Jesus sees them – clothed in his righteousness.

CHAPTER 9

The long arm of the law

GALATIANS 3:10-14

Aim: To gain a further understanding of what Christ has done for us by setting us free from the restraints of the law

FOCUS ON THE THEME:
'I parked my car and began walking up the street. Then I suddenly heard a shout. Turning, I saw a policeman. My first thought was, what have I done? My car was taxed and insured. . . I hadn't parked in the wrong place, had I? My mouth went dry in any case. 'Hi!' said the policeman. Then I realised – it was my friend's brother, someone I hadn't seen for a long time. He just wanted a chat. I was so glad to see a friend instead of having to face the full effects of a law I might have broken. . . wouldn't you be?'

Reading: Galatians 3:10-14
Key verse: Galatians 3:13

A friend of mine recently acquired too many points on his licence from the same speed camera. Result? He's not driving at the moment! Imagine a world where not only your car driving but your every move was caught on camera 24/7, like the kind of nightmare envisaged in George Orwell's book *1984*. You don't need to imagine it: welcome to the world of 'law keeping' as the road to personal salvation.

At one level, these verses are not easy. Words, phrases and allusions are used that presume we know our Old Testaments well: 'law', 'cursed', 'the righteous', 'the blessing given to Abraham' etc. However, at another level, they simply raise the central question of the Bible: how can anyone be right with God?

Yogi Berra, the legendary New York Yankees baseball pitcher of a previous generation, is equally famous for his 'Yogi-isms.' Here's one of them: 'When you come to a fork in the road, take it!' Funny, but rather unhelpful when we need to know the right road to God. Which is right?

A FORK IN THE ROAD

There can be few people who are not confused by the multiplicity of religions, major faiths, DIY New Age cults etc that are on offer in the western world today. Who's right? Where is exclusive truth, if such there be, to be found? These verses offer two systems that summarise our choices.

There's hardly a religion in the world that would not want to affirm some 'agreed on all sides' truth: there must be more to life than the merely biological; purpose and meaning are possible because there is someone/something bigger than we humans. So, there's probably an after-life etc. Accordingly, join that group, live this way, do your best and hopefully this world and the next will be better as a result. Although Paul's comments are originally aimed at the opponents of the gospel in his day, they graphically illustrate the near universal religious belief: 'the man who does these things will live by them' (v12). Note the two verbs, 'does' and 'live.' If we want to 'live', the deal is that we 'do' (Lev. 18:5). The question arises, how much do we need to 'do' to be sure we will 'live'? Some religions say that at the end of time God will weigh our good and bad actions on his scales: pray they tip in your favour. Just the other day, I was chatting to one of our graduates from Moorlands who came to Christ from another religion. What drove his search was the vision of those scales in the hands of God. What alarmed him regularly was the question, 'What if the scales are perfectly balanced?' What would be his fate then?

In contrast to the 'do, do, do' of religion, Paul says 'the righteous will live by faith' (v11, quoting Habakkuk 2:4). This statement is not only a contrast to 'do' but an antithesis, the very opposite. This is another way altogether, but more of that route presently. In the meanwhile, another road presents itself.

● *In times gone by, many evangelists preached hellfire and brimstone but we don't do that too much today. Why not? How do you think negating the existence of a lost eternity can give people a false picture of what happens when they die? How can we begin to speak the truth in love without denying Jesus' own teaching on what will happen to those who do not trust in him for salvation?*

THE ROAD TO RUIN

As we have seen elsewhere, the group Paul was opposing are known as the Judaisers. They wanted Gentile believers to become Jewish in their customs and practices. They were the ones who 'rely on', 'continue to do', the laws of God (v10), in the belief that they 'will live by them' (v12). Does that sound reasonable? It might do until one begins to ask what 'observing the law' might entail. Take the Ten Commandments. Are they like an exam paper: only five out of ten to be attempted? Do you recall the first one, 'No other gods before me'? Do you know anyone who has kept that 24/7? But this is only the start of our problems. Remember the Rabbis computed that there are 613 laws; 365 'Thou shalt nots' and 248 'Thou shalts.' Can you name them? Ignorance of them is neither bliss nor excuse. And if you can enumerate them, then the challenge is 'to do everything written in the Book of the Law' (v10, see Deuteronomy 27:26). And just in case anyone starts getting smug – 'I've done my best, better than most' – Jesus, in the Sermon on the Mount, reminds us that keeping the law is not merely an outward affair. We can just as easily commit murder or adultery in thought as in deed (Mt. 5:21-28), for the law weighs motives as well as deeds. The law has a very long arm: it touches every part of life, 'everything written' (v10). And when we fail, we are 'under a curse' (v10), the judgement of God.

It is easy to feel this is all so unfair. People do their best, rise to the challenge and then are condemned. Why even try? Without pre-empting the content of the next paragraphs (especially verses 19-20), we need to realise how perverse the human heart can be. When God gave his law to ancient Israel, a new temptation was introduced. It is called 'legalism.' As we have elsewhere noted, legalism is not the same as being organised, reading your Bible, saying your prayers, going to church, tithing your income etc. Legalism is when you 'rely on' (v10) anyone or anything other than Jesus Christ for salvation. Why? Because 'no-one is justified before God by the law' (v11) for the simple reason that no-one, save Christ, has ever fully kept it. At this point, it would be good to read Romans 3:19,20 where we are reminded that the law silences every mouth. Indeed, one way to tell if someone is a Christian is to ask how they are expecting to get into heaven. Very quickly they give their game away. If someone's talk is about 'All I've done, achieved, merited, deserved', you can be sure they are operating on a law basis: their 'mouth' has not been silenced. God 'owes' them. The truth is that God owes no-one anything. If he did, then grace would not be grace. Law keeping without Jesus is the road to perdition. There's another way.

● *Can you think of an example where people might be tempted to trust in their works? Do you think people who have been mightily used by God could be more susceptible to this kind of deception?*

THE CROSS ROAD

'The curse of the law' (v13) is ultimately the judgment of and separation from God. It is, if I may put it this way, 'Karma' – you reap what you sow, which means 'death' (Rom. 6:23). That's why it was easy to spot a serious law-breaker in the Old Testament: 'Cursed is everyone who is hung on a tree' (3:13 from Deuteronomy 21:23). You could look and say, 'He got what was coming to him.' But note the astonishing language used here: Christ became 'a curse for us . . . hung on a tree' (v13). Did Jesus get 'what was coming to him'? No, he got what was coming to us, 'a curse for us' (v13).

This view of the cross, 'a curse for us', has traditionally been part of the doctrine known as penal substitutionary atonement. Simply expressed, it tells us that all that was the due penalty for sin has been paid by an innocent substitute, the Son of God himself (4:4f). In the past, some have dismissed this view of the cross as the 'language of the butcher's shop' and more recently as a form of 'cosmic child abuse.' Of course, it is not the only model of atonement the Bible expresses, but it is a central one. Jesus himself said he came to 'give his life as a ransom for (literally 'instead of') many' (Mk. 10:45). Centuries before, Isaiah prophesied that 'the Lord has laid on him the iniquity of us all' (Is. 53:6). One of my favourite illustrations of this truth is found in the life of Schamyl.

Schamyl was the great leader and champion of his people's freedom. For thirty years, he confounded Russian advancement in the Caucasus. After a most adventurous life, he died in 1871. At one period of his rule, bribery and corruption were so prevalent that he passed a draconian law. Every case discovered would carry a penalty of a hundred lashes of the whip. Not long after, a culprit was discovered – his own mother!

The great leader shut himself away in his tent. What should he do? Make an exception for his mother? If so, then how would he ever again stand before his people as a lawgiver and man of his word? His law was given to curb evil and for his people's benefit. Punish her? That was unthinkable. She would doubtlessly die under the punishment. How could he satisfy both his law and his love?

After two days, he emerged from his tent and ordered a public flogging of his mother. Once, twice . . . five times the whip tore in to her back and took the flesh from it. Then Schamyl stepped in, cut her down, had himself strung up, bared his back and directed the guard to inflict the remaining punishment upon him. He believed he had satisfied both his justice, since the hundred lashes had been met, and his love, for his mother went free.

Illustrations are capable of highlighting or distorting the truth. Rightly, the story of Schamyl and his mother illustrates both the justice and love of God. The distortion would be the deduction that on the cross Jesus suffered *most* of our punishment. The incredible story of the gospel is that he has become 'a curse for us.' The cross of Jesus fully satisfies the justice and love of God. If the cross is enough for God, it ought to be enough for you and me.

So, by the death of Jesus we are 'redeemed' (v13). We are freed by a new master, who has 'bought us at a price' (1 Cor. 6:20), incredibly his own 'precious blood' (1 Pet. 1:19). And this was God's purpose all along, in order that Abraham's blessing, that is, being justified (v8) and receiving a new life, 'the promise of the Spirit' (v14), may come to us, whether we are Jew or Gentile.

How does this happen? Law relies on what I can *do*; faith relies on what Christ has *done*. Here we really are at the ultimate cross road. Religion basically runs on the idea of 'karma': you reap what you sow, you get what you deserve. In effect, you rely upon yourself and save yourself. But grace comes along and changes all that. It interrupts and diverts the consequences of my actions to Christ. In this context, faith is nothing other than laying hold of and relying on Jesus Christ alone as Saviour and Lord.

In his famous poem *The Road not Taken*, Robert Frost spoke of the less travelled road that made all the difference. The road to ruin has more speed cameras than we can imagine. The road to God is full of mercy where the righteous may live (and drive!) by grace. Who would want to be caught by the long arm of the law when we can be saved by the strong hand of the Lord?

FURTHER READING
Look at one or all of the accounts of the crucifixion in the Gospels. Spend some time in silent meditation and then praise God for his wonderful gift.

REFLECTION AND RESPONSE
- You are bought at a price . . . a very great price. Some people may wonder at how God could possibly allow his Son to go through it, but we must take a different view. God himself, in Jesus, chose to pay the price. Jesus is 'God in a body' (Col. 2:9). Why did he do

this? Because of his great love for each one of us. It's all about *his* love, not *our* ability to please him.

• Jesus became a curse for us so we might have Abraham's blessing. It is all done; there is nothing more to do. Jesus has done it all for us! We are free. Think about that freedom.

SMALL GROUP DISCUSSION POINT
You might like to share a communion meal as you remember what Jesus has done for you.

CHAPTER 10

Where there's a will . . .

GALATIANS 3:15-22

Aim: To consider the purpose of the law, the covenant fulfilled in Christ and the freedom he brings us

FOCUS ON THE THEME:
Have you ever tried washing your car with a dirty rag? You simply can't make a dirty car clean by using a dirty cloth. This is a useful picture of the futility of trying to make ourselves 'good' in God's sight! What else do we do? Brainstorm some ideas.

Reading: Galatians 3:15-22
Key verse: Galatians 3:22

Those in the legal profession know how to complete our chapter title, 'Where there's a will . . . there's a relative.' It's based on the rather depressing observation that family members, unseen or unheard of for years, appear out of the woodwork when a relative has died.

At one level, Paul is playing the role of a lawyer presiding at the reading of a will. Who are the rightful beneficiaries? Who is going to get their hands on the family estate? According to his opponents, it was obvious. It is those who 'rely on observing the law' (v10). They would have conceded that faith in Jesus was important too. But at rock bottom that was not adequate: more was needed than simply trusting oneself to Christ and living accordingly. In reality, when the deal is Jesus Christ plus something else, it is something else that becomes the focus for faith and obedience. In their case, it was the law. In that case, 'Christ died for nothing' (2:21).

Into these eight verses are telescoped two thousand years of biblical history and three giants of the faith; Abraham, Moses and Jesus. You may recall that Abraham was living as a pagan in Ur of the Chaldees when God called him to leave all that behind, and he did (Gen. 12:1-4). To him, God unconditionally made promises to bless him and his descendants, his 'seed' (Gal. 3:16). Abraham was, as someone has put it, merely an 'astonished bystander.' God said, 'I will, I will, I will', and all Abraham had to do was say, 'Thank you!' It is like some hoodie living in a sink estate called to a lawyer's office to be told that an unknown relative in another part of the world has died and left her multi-million dollar estate to him. How can he know? Because it is in her last will and testament. What does he need to do? In one sense, nothing. Simply believe the good news, receive the estate and, hopefully, let it so change his life for the better from here on. Imagine, however, that a year or two after the young man has received his inheritance, someone challenges the will. 'It does not really belong to you at all. There's someone far more deserving, so give back your estate.'

Here's something of the problem Paul is confronting. The Judaisers were challenging 'the will.' How does Paul respond? He does so by taking us through the meaning of covenant, the purpose of the law and the freedom found in Christ.

THE COVENANT'S FINALITY

Paul has some hard things to say in these verses but he introduces them with the word 'Brothers' (v15), even though he started the chapter describing them as 'foolish' (v1). It is an important point to remember, when we are embroiled in some theological or church debate, that we are dealing with the family of God. He proceeds to give 'an everyday illustration' (JBP) drawn from 'a human covenant' (v15). The word we translate as 'covenant' could equally be rendered 'will', or 'testament', the word we use in referring to the Old or New Testament.

In the Greek world of his day, Paul knew that once someone had made a will, it could not be changed. However, during the same period, if one's will was made under Roman law, it could be changed, very much as in English law today. But it matters little whether the background is Roman or Greek. Once a will has been ratified and the testator has died, 'no-one can set aside or add' to it (v15). We know, of course, from both history and experience that many have tried. In my wider family network, a distant relative attempted to do just that. She was not very popular with the rest of the family! It was illegal. It was not allowed and rightly so. The testator had in mind her beneficiaries and they were the ones who were to share her estate. Her last will and testament said so.

Likewise, runs Paul's argument, the promises made by God's covenant/will to Abraham are not abrogated or superseded by the law which came hundreds of years later (the starting date of '430 years' (v17) is probably from the time of Jacob). That law cannot 'do away with the promise' (v17). Note that word 'promise', it occurs seven times in these verses. In the Bible there are two kinds of promise, conditional and unconditional. If it is the former, you do your part of the agreement and God does his. But this covenant promise to Abraham is not like that. It is unconditional, it is a covenant of sheer grace (v18), in which God takes the initiative to bestow an inheritance that does not depend on law but promise (v18). So here's the application: those who belong to the 'seed . . . Christ' (v16) are the beneficiaries of the inheritance God has promised.

For the analogy to hold, of course, a testator must die because 'a will is in force only when somebody has died' (Heb. 9:17). So who has died? 'For this reason Christ is the mediator of a new covenant . . . now that he has died as a ransom to set them free' (Heb. 9:15). When God gave his covenant promise to bless Abraham, he knew the cost, the death of his own Son, 'cursed . . . hung on a tree' (v13). So why the law?

● *Read in Genesis 15 about the blood covenant God made with Abraham. God made the covenant. . . and God put himself on oath as he passed through the pieces (v17). What can we learn of the integrity of God's nature as we read this passage and consider how the promise was fulfilled in the New Testament?*

THE LAW'S PURPOSE

The riposte of Paul's opponents in Galatia undoubtedly is echoed here. 'Paul, you're making God's law redundant. How dare you!' Paul, in reply, makes three points about the law: what it indicates, why it is inferior and what it is incapable of doing.

Firstly, the law 'was added because of transgressions' (v19). Some interpret that to mean the law was given as a brake, a restraint until the coming of Jesus. So, for example, the Mosaic legislation on divorce was not to encourage divorce but to restrain the hardness of people's hearts (Mk. 10:5). The law certainly can do that. Another interpretation goes further. Law makes 'wrongdoing a legal offence' (NEB: Rom. 4:15, 5:20). It was probably always wrong and irresponsible to drive at 120 mph, but until the 70 mph speed limit was imposed, it was not a legal offence. When God's law came along, it categorised sin, it specified our 'transgression', the place we had transgressed the line (or speed limit). The law shows sin in all its heinous and horrible hues.

In my teens, over forty years ago, I started reading the Bible. I ploughed through it nearly twice, beginning at Genesis. Before I started, I felt pretty good about myself. When I finished, I felt like Robert Murray M'Cheyne expressed it in a verse from his hymn, *I once was a stranger*

> When free grace awoke me,
> By light from on high,
> Then legal fears shook me,
> I trembled to die.

The law can show me how very rotten to the core I am. But herein lies the perversity of human nature. As Andrew Jukes put it: 'Satan would have us prove ourselves holy by the law which God gave to prove us sinners.' That is precisely, I believe, at the heart of Paul's debate with the Judaisers.

There's a second thing about the law: it is inferior to the promise. Why? Because it is both temporary and indirect. It is temporary 'until the Seed' (v19), Christ, should come. It is indirect because it was 'put into effect through angels by a mediator' (v19). So, by the time it reached the people it was third-hand. I get a call from my local MP who has heard from a Cabinet Minister that the Prime Minister wants me to pay twice as much tax. That's a little different to a direct call on my mobile from someone who says, 'Hi, Steve, Gordon here!' In the gospel, God in Christ speaks to us directly: 'the promise of God needs neither angelic witness nor human intermediary but depends on him alone' (v20, JBP).

The third thing about the law is its inability to 'impart life' (v21). Recently, I invested in a Sat Nav for my car. The calm voice of the 'lady' directs my journeys all over the UK. If I miss a turning she will tell me and gently re-route me. She does have one very annoying habit, however: creep a mile or two over a speed limit, and she lets me know: 'You are exceeding the speed limit . . . You are exceeding . . . ' She tells me what is right, what is wrong, and directs and re-directs me. But that's all. My Sat Nav has never got me anywhere. It's my car, via its engine, that has provided the power. Likewise, the law cannot give what it demands, 'righteousness' (v21). For that I need Jesus.

● *The law can tell you where you are wrong but it can't help you out of the mess. Before we knew we needed help, God already had a plan. How does knowing he was answering your need before you even realised you had one increase your faith in God for everyday provision?*

FREEDOM IN CHRIST

The world we live in has some 6.2 billion people, probably 250 times more people than Paul's day. Despite all our differences, one thing we all have in common is that we are part of a world that is 'a prisoner of sin' (v22). Many don't realise that life is a gaol, that at every turn there are barred windows and heavily locked doors that restrain us. No-one is ultimately free. More worrying still, we are all on Death Row. One day we will be judged by our Maker. The law of God only confirms our sentence. But when we are awakened, we begin to cry out for pardon and release. Then, one day we hear footsteps coming down the corridor and the prison door is opened wide. A man walks in who is different to anyone we have ever met. He is carrying a royal pardon for 'those who believe' him (v22). We note that his hands are pierced, his brow scarred, marks of the 'faith(fulness) . . . of Jesus Christ' (v22) to 'death on a tree' (v13). The cell is irradiated by his presence, his love and his invitation to 'Come, follow me.' 'What was promised' (v22) for centuries through the 'seed . . . who is Christ' (v16) is now available: redemption, life, righteousness, inheritance etc. If one word sums up what Christ has provided for our freedom, that word is 'everything.' Such a picture seems to have been in the mind of Charles Wesley in his famous hymn, *And can it be*

> Long my imprisoned spirit lay
> Fast bound in sin and nature's night;
> Thine eye diffused a quickening ray,
> I woke the dungeon flamed with light;
> My chains fell off, my heart was free;
> I rose, went forth, and followed Thee.

Wesley's next verse says, 'No condemnation now I dread.' Why? Because there is no condemnation for 'those who believe . . . in Jesus Christ' (v22). Imagine that hoodie referred to earlier wanting to stay just as he was and where he was, when he now had the opportunity for a new life. The Liberator has come to set captives free, to take us out of our spiritual 'sink estates' into the 'glorious freedom of the children of God' (Rom. 8:21). Don't leave life without him!

FURTHER STUDY

Read Hebrews 9 as you consider the blood covenant God has made with his people. Christ is the 'mediator of [the] new covenant . . . he has died as a ransom to set [us] free' (v15). Before a will can be brought into effect, the one who made the will must die. So Jesus' death brought into effect the terms of his will – that is, the new covenant. Then Jesus came back to make sure his was carried out.

REFLECTION AND RESPONSE
Are you walking in the freedom of the gospel, or has someone or something taken that freedom away? What constructive steps can you take to walk in his grace again?

SMALL GROUP DISCUSSION POINT
Use your direct access to the throne of grace to intercede for each other and pray for the needs of your fellowship.

CHAPTER 11

God's forever family

GALATIANS 3:23-29

Aim: To see ourselves as children of destiny

FOCUS ON THE THEME:
Write 'black' 'white' 'male' 'female' 'outcast' and 'slave' on
different pieces of paper. Slip them inside your Bible. This is a
good illustration to show that we are all hidden in Christ
and co-heirs, regardless of race, sex or status. Think about
historical figures born to rule, that were imprisoned or
outcasts for a time. Do you think they ever lost heart, when
all seemed bleak? Or did their trust in their God-given
destiny sustain them? How can this sustain us when we go
through hard times?

Reading: Galatians 3:23-29
Key verse: Galatians 3:28

Recently, furore erupted over alleged racialist remarks
made against a Bollywood star by other contestants in the
Celebrity Big Brother house. Questions were raised in
Parliament, Gordon Brown, the then Chancellor, had to
apologise whilst in India, but Channel 4 TV decided to let
the programme continue! Each month continues to witness
hundreds of deaths caused by the internecine strife of Sunni
and Shia factions in Iraq, fuelled by American and others'
presence there. John Lennon's *Imagine* dreamt of a world
where we could all live as one, free from evil and prejudice.

Is this possible, in a world dominated by racialism, sexual exploitation and economic injustice?

Welcome to the vision we glimpse in this section. In essence, these verses describe what the Kingdom of God looks like. Here is the alternative society, the counter-culture, God's great antidote for human fragmentation, brokenness and alienation. It is the place where love abounds, because we 'are all one in Christ Jesus' (v28). Welcome, it says, to the . . . wait for it! . . . Church! Oh no! Well, here's an alternative phrase: Welcome to God's forever family, where all are 'sons of God through faith in Jesus Christ' (v26). How does that occur? Via a 'before', a 'through' and a 'because of' Jesus.

● *'Great, I've met Jesus. He's alive. Oh no! That means I'll have to go to church!' In what ways can 'church' seem a daunting proposition to those who have become new converts? Is there any way we can make 'church' more accessible ?*

BEFORE JESUS – IN CUSTODY (23-25)

Paul's seemingly depressing picture of life without Christ – bondage, imprisonment – is strangely encouraging. I recall too many occasions when I had not completed my homework, and yet felt better because I discovered that half of my classmates had not done so either. We were all 'condemned', but at least we were in the same boat. 'Before this faith came . . . until faith should be revealed' (v23) are ways of speaking of the coming of Christ. What was life like before? Well, 'we were held prisoners by the law' (v23). The word translated 'prisoner' here is a strong term – guarded, policed. It was used, for instance, of placing a military garrison around a town to ensure someone, Paul in this instance, did not escape (2 Cor. 11:32). Have you ever been in a prison cell? A while ago, a prisoner in custody asked that a Baptist minister visit him. I was the nearest the authorities could get to the real deal. I spent a little over half an hour in that cell with him. It was warm enough, but claustrophobic and sparsely furnished, with few creature comforts. Worst of all, of course, when it was time to go, I had to leave my new friend to the barred windows and the clunk of that heavy steel door and the turning of the lock. I'd been inside before – always professionally, I hasten to add – but the awfulness of life on the inside, even for a few minutes, dawned on me afresh. I was free to leave, to go where I wanted when I wanted. The prisoner wasn't.

The other phrase, 'locked up' (v23), is translated 'prisoner' in verse 22. The word underlying our translation is used of 'locking up' a great shoal of fish – see Luke 5:6. It's a graphic picture. Fish are caught in a net, hemmed in, imprisoned. And the amazing thing about this gaol is that it is the law that is the gaoler! It is not the law's fault, for it is 'holy, righteous and good' (Rom. 7:12). Rather, the problem lies in the human heart, which is sick, sad and deceitful (Jer. 17:9).

Years ago, there was a debate in the letters column of *The Times* newspaper about what was wrong with the world. The shortest letter *The Times* has ever published was written by the famous G.K. Chesterton: 'Sir, I am, Yours, G.K. Chesterton.' Take the question of injustice in the world. It has been computed that everyone on planet Earth could annually be fed, clothed, housed, educated and cared for medically for the same amount we spend militarily every two weeks.

But the law has another function, a marvellous one, 'to lead us to Christ' (v24). The word underlying this translation gives us the English word 'pedagogue', literally a 'leader of a boy.' In Paul's day, the 'pedagogue' would be a household servant whose task it was to look after his master's son between the ages of around seven to eighteen, Junior School to Sixth Form today. He was not the boy's teacher. His role was to ensure he was taught, so he got him to school on time etc. He could be like a 'strict governess' (JBP), a sergeant-major for discipline, though he would also act as a bodyguard if the boy's life was in danger. In a real sense, the whole of the Old Testament functions like this. It is our 'pedagogue': every part of it, every book is part of a bigger story, the meta-narrative to use the jargon, and that story, expressed in law, prophecy, pain, failure and anticipation, is all pointing to and longing for its fulfilment and finale, the coming of the Messiah, Jesus.

● *'Even if someone does not know anything about Christianity and has scant knowledge of the Ten Commandments, they have an inbuilt sense of right and wrong.' What might stifle or even extinguish a natural sense of knowing we have done something 'wrong', even before we know about the law? Can a person who has consistently hardened their heart to 'right and wrong' ever be reached for the gospel?*

THROUGH JESUS – INTO LIBERTY

The period of preparation has been eclipsed by the time of fulfilment. So, 'before this faith came' (v23), is contrasted with 'now that faith has come' (v25). Of course, there was 'faith' before Jesus came (vs 6,11), for the Old Testament bears witness to 'the prophets, who spoke of the grace that was to come' by those who had 'the Spirit of Christ in them' (1 Pet.1:10-12). But now, the full story of God's intentions in Christ has had its 'apocalypse' ('revealed', v23). The law was a staging post, part of the journey, but Christ is the journey's end, the 'telos', the goal and purpose of the law

(Rom. 10:4). Now we are 'justified by faith' (v24) and consequently no longer under the 'supervision (pedagogue) of the law' (v25). Rather, we 'are all sons of God' (v26) which means, in terms of spiritual chronology, we are no longer at the infant or adolescent stage of revelation (Gal. 4:1-7) but at the mature stage: Christ has come. And lest some of us find 'sons' to sound non-inclusive, a good reason for its retention is that it echoes the Old Testament's language of inheritance rights. Consequently, 'male' and 'female' (v28) are equally 'heirs' (v29).

Within its context, the foregoing was at the heart of Paul's trouble with the Judaisers. They insisted that maturity could only be realised by making 'pagans' into 'Jews' via circumcision. They wanted to keep these believers as spiritual Peter Pans and Wendys in the NeverNeverLand of spiritual adolescence, via the law with its multitude of obligations. It's as if Christ had not come with his full blinding revelation and redemptive power. So Paul vigorously insisted that in Christ alone could spiritual life and maturity be found and maintained.

So, is this simply a long forgotten theological battle with little to say to us? Hardly. Many years ago, I asked a mainly Protestant congregation in Northern Ireland, at the height of the Troubles there, whether a Roman Catholic had to become a Protestant in order to become a born again Christian. You could hear a pin drop. Far from my losing my grip on the evangelical faith, I was concerned that some folk seemed more interested in their Protestant political hegemony, and all its cultural trappings and baggage, than for nominal Catholics or Protestants to experience the Lord Jesus personally. Similarly, in some forms of evangelical fundamentalism, we know who are the truly 'saved' by what they don't do rather than by what they do and are in Christ.

There are three things I must not do –
Booze and 'baccy or cinema queue.
And there's one more – I won't take a chance –
Oh, Lord forbid, that I should dance!

I know there are reasons for avoiding all the above. But anything that obscures the centrality of Christ and threatens to take me back to mere rules and regulations is 'Life BC' – before Christ.

In contrast, 'sons of God' is what we are now in Christ. God is our Father, Christ our Elder Brother, and we are family and 'heirs according to the promise' (v29). How staggering that is. You will only need one second in heaven to know that a lifetime on a throne as a King or Queen, reigning over a vast domain, repeated a thousand times over, is as nothing compared 'with the glory that will be revealed in us' (Rom. 8:18).

So how does one get in and stay in the family of God? This was at the heart of the Judaisers' challenge. It is still as relevant today when we talk of Christian initiation and discipleship. The Judaisers may have agreed that we get into the family of God by 'grace', however defined (v18). But to stay in, that required 'law', especially the ceremonial laws of 'special days' etc (4:10), and, of course, circumcision. In contrast, Paul says repeatedly that it is through 'faith/believing', used about fifteen times in this chapter alone. In addition, Paul uses a word that today could scupper any possibility of demonstrating that Christians are 'all one in Christ Jesus' (v28), the motto of the worldwide Keswick Convention. That word is 'baptism.'

Two opposites concerning baptism should immediately be addressed. One side says that what baptism symbolises, death to sin and being alive to God (Rom. 6:3,4), actually happens precisely through baptism. This is Christian initiation via baptismal regeneration, and can therefore be administered to both children and adults. The opposite view is that baptism is merely a symbol and is not obligatory, so setting aside both Christ's commands and apostolic practice. More surefooted, I believe, is the summation of the Book of Common Prayer to the effect that the sacraments, baptism included, are an 'outward and visible sign of an inward and spiritual grace.' In the New Testament it was the outward corollary of faith in Christ. When Paul was told to 'be baptised . . . calling on his name' (Acts 22:16), we are reminded that baptism is an 'acted prayer', an 'appeal to God for a clear conscience' (1 Pet. 3:21, RSV). The 'normal Christian birth' includes repentance toward God, faith in Jesus, water baptism and reception of the Spirit. Two thousand years of Church history have often divided what God has joined together. Whatever your stance on water baptism, the mark of a child of God is being 'clothed . . . with Christ' (v27), the spiritual reality of Jesus covering our sin, guilt and shame with his righteousness, grace and love. Welcome to the family!

- *How important is it to walk in Christ's redemptive power for 'life in abundance', as promised by Jesus in John 10:10b?*
- *Read Ephesians 1:15-23. What does Paul pray for the Ephesians that we could very well pray for ourselves – and for other Christians?*

BECAUSE OF JESUS – IN THE FAMILY

The implications of verse 28 are so staggering that neither the Church nor society have yet worked them all through practically. Race, economic structures and gender issues are addressed here in three telling phrases.

Take the first, 'neither Jew nor Greek.' The ancient world was awash with racialism. Jews looked down on 'Gentile dogs', Greeks dismissed non-Greeks as 'barbarians' and Jews as 'atheists' because they did not believe in their pantheon of gods, but only one God. Like all sin, racialism flows from pride that assumes we are better than others and ignorance that does not know, or chooses to forget, that from one man, Adam, God 'made every nation of men' (Acts 17:26).

What about 'slave nor free'? This year 2007 is, thank God, the 200th Anniversary in Great Britain of the abolition of the slave trade, that blot on British history of appalling inhumanity and cruelty to fellow human beings (and Britain was not the worst offender). But to even a cultured Greek like the philosopher Aristotle, slaves were merely 'animated implements' or 'breathing tools.' Though many masters were kind and generous, others were callous and capricious, especially and perversely those who had been slaves themselves. Is that because, generally speaking, hurt people hurt people?

With regard to the 'battle of the sexes', it is as old as humankind (Gen. 3). One Jewish prayer daily thanked God not to have been born a Gentile dog, a woman or a slave. Even the great historian Josephus wrote that 'Woman, so says the law, is inferior in all things.' Male chauvinism has a long and ignoble history.

Here are the marks of the world we still inhabit: racialism, class exploitation and sexism with all their attendant miseries. So, people are judged and excluded by the colour of their skin rather than the content of their character, to echo Martin Luther King; children become economic slaves in sweatshops of the Third World or sexual slaves in brothels in Cambodia and Thailand; women (and men!) are battered and damaged (and sometimes murdered) by abusive partners. And then the Liberator comes. He says to everyone, regardless of religion, race, rank or sexual gender, 'Come, 'belong' (v29) to me.' Here is equality in the sight of God for anyone and everyone who has 'faith in Christ Jesus' (v26). Regardless of our background, culture, economic status, age or gender, we are welcome. However dysfunctional your earthly family was/is, or no matter how good, here is the ultimate family with a Father who has ever loved us and always will, a Brother who is always on our side and in our corner, and a family Comforter who will never leave us.

We must not think Paul was being naïve. He knew these divisions in humanity still existed, as they do in abundance in our world. His point was not to pretend that these categories had disappeared. Rather, he was insistent that, in Christ, these distinctions do not matter any more as an entry requirement for getting in and staying in God's family. When we belong to Christ, we are 'Abraham's seed, and heirs according to promise' (v29). A Christian is an heir. However tragic, broken, unloved and dreadful a fellow Christian's life has been, no matter what baggage and scars she carries still, if we could glimpse her just for a moment as she will be on resurrection morning, a 'co-heir with Christ' (Rom. 8:17), 'like him' (1 Jn. 3:2) forever, we would treat her with the respect we would show to a queen. Guess what? That's precisely how the Lord would have us treat others in his forever family now. So at the local church level, let's celebrate our diversity and thank God for our unity, 'all one in Christ Jesus' (v28). And the Lord won't mind your seeing yourself in that light of glory either: you are a prince, a princess, waiting for your King. Lift up your head, remember you belong to Christ, you are part of a worldwide family stretching back into eternity, rooted in history and headed for an incredible destiny. Go and face your world as a child of God today!

FURTHER READING

Read Revelation 21 and 22. What a wonderful future we have as members of heaven's royal family!

REFLECTION AND RESPONSE

- How can knowing who we really are – a member of heaven's royalty with a glorious future – help to sustain us when life seems hard? If you are going through a difficult time at present, read again the last two chapters of Revelation and allow God to minister his strength and peace to your spirit. Know that all things pass, and there is a wonderful ending.

- Horrifically, sex trade slavery is still alive and well in the twenty-first century. Pray about how you can become involved in putting an end to this vile practice, perhaps by contacting an organisation such as Stop the Traffik.

SMALL GROUP DISCUSSION POINT

Look again at Focus on the Theme. It is a humbling and yet exhilarating experience to think we are all one in Christ Jesus. Spend time praying for anyone who feels their background/status or gender is a barrier to being a co- heir in Christ. Pray too for anyone known to you who has a fractured background and is in need of support from their church family. How can you help them practically this week?

CHAPTER 12

A God named Abba

GALATIANS 4:1-11

Aim: To encourage us to live as children of our heavenly Father

FOCUS ON THE THEME:
Earlier in our study, we thought about the example of the hoodie who suddenly found himself rich – but then had to go back to the way he lived before. But what if the hoodie hadn't found his inheritance challenged . . . yet made the choice to return to a futile lifestyle of drug addiction and promiscuity on a sink estate? It would be a very real waste, wouldn't it? Why do you think the temptation to return to a former, less successful, way of life is so compelling?

Reading: Galatians 4:1-11
Key verses: Galatians 4:6,7,9

What is the greatest threat to Christian faith today? No-one should underestimate the growth of secularism or the popularity of atheistic theories of life represented by the likes of Richard Dawkins' *The God Delusion*. It would be folly to believe that totalitarian communism is dead and buried: check out North Korea. But there is a far more subtle threat. It is religion.

The heart of Christianity is beautifully expressed in this section: 'Now that you know God – or rather are known by God' (v9). A dear old friend of mine, when she was alive, was a 'royalist' to the core of her being: she loved the Royal Family and knew so much about the Queen via books, TV programmes etc. Her problem was twofold, however. She did not *know* the Queen personally and Her Majesty did not know her. In contrast, through the gospel, we come to know and be known of God. Yes, of course, God 'knows' everyone and everything! Here, however, is the language of relationship and intimacy, 'Abba, Father' (v6).

● *How could you most effectively explain to a new Christian the difference between 'knowing' Christ and 'knowing about' him?*
● *Why do you think 'religion' – that is, Christian-based 'religion' – is a subtle threat to knowing Christ?*

Both in Paul's day and ours, religion, expressed in a multitude of forms, can 'enslave' (v9) people, whilst denying them the experience of 'the Spirit of his Son' in their hearts (v6). It was such a threat to Christian liberty that Paul faced here. So, he reminds them of what they were (1-3) who they are (4-7) and what they must not do – become enslaved again (8-11).

REMEMBER WHEN YOU WERE A 'NIPPER'? (1-3)

Bear with the slang, 'nipper.' But it's the closest I can get to giving you the Greek word used for 'child/children' used here. A 'nepios', literally 'not speaking', is a young child and the practice Paul refers to in the Greco-Roman world of his day has parallels to our own. A father has an eye to the future of his child, so he sets up a trust fund for him. But he is a wise father. If the child inherits 'the whole estate' (v1) whilst still in infancy, there may be little or nothing to show when he reaches maturity. When my own children were 'nippers' we had our first visit to Disneyworld, Florida. If it had been possible for them to get their hands on any inheritance coming their way, they would gladly have cashed it in and gone to live with Mickey Mouse in Disneyworld (they would have had enough for about three days, I reckon). So, Brenda, my wife, and I took a precautionary step. With a Christian couple who had similarly aged children, we entered into a mutual agreement to be each others' 'guardians and trustees' (v2) in the event of either set of parents dying whilst our families were still quite young. (This is something many parents should consider). Our children, Paul and Ruth, would be cared for if we died, but any residual inheritance would await 'the time set' (v3) by us, in this case, when they reached twenty-one.

Paul applies an analogy like this to the spiritual biography of the Galatians. There was a time 'when we were children . . . in slavery under the basic principles of the world' (v3). 'Principles' carries the idea of 'elementary instruction' or the 'ABC' of something. In the context here, it appears to mean elementary rules and regulations. It is 'Do and do, do and do, rule on rule, rule on rule; a little here, a little there' (Is. 28:10). It is 'basic moral principles' (JBP). If the 'we' is pressed, Paul may be referring to his own Jewish culture primarily. He was given a moral framework from God's law. If 'world' is emphasised, then it is the kind of instruction that any culture may provide to form children into adults. Both emphases may be present. Whether one's background is Jewish or Greek, Christian or pagan, this period before personal faith in Jesus Christ still leaves us in a spiritual kindergarten stage: 'children . . . in slavery' (v3). Whatever gracious designs a father may have for his child, the child 'is no different from a slave . . . although he owns the whole estate' (v1).

Herein lies both the power and limits of religion and morality. Both may produce good and decent citizens, preferable indeed to a criminal underclass or the reign of anarchy. But in terms of putting people right with their Maker, it is all too possible for people to live as 'slaves' to a moral or religious system and never experience being a son of God. Recently, a local vicar who has been running an Alpha Course in his rather traditional church told me, 'Steve, it's been super. Folk have been saying things like, "Vicar, I didn't realise I could actually speak to Jesus for myself."' Conversely, a friend was lamenting the fact that his eighty-year-old mother still believed that her church attendance, penance and prayers would do the trick for getting her into heaven, and just could not see why she needed Jesus. She seemed to prefer the 'church of perpetual obligation' to the spiritual 'land of the free.' And you? Still a 'nipper' or a son?

● *Spend some time thinking about your life since you met Christ. Can you see how much you have changed and grown in your faith? Write down anything that comes to mind in a journal and diary. Sometimes casting an eye over our journey so far can encourage us to keep going!*

IT'S CHRISTMAS . . . ! (4-7)

A favourite Church history exam question for generations of theological students ran along the lines of 'Christianity was born into a world that favoured its growth. Discuss.' The more diligent students would be able to produce the classic answers about 'when the time had fully come' (v4). Greek language and culture had given a common tongue to the Roman world, which in turn had brought the Pax Romana, with its excellent roads and legal and communication systems. In addition, the Jewish faith had synagogues throughout the Empire and a translation of its

Scriptures into Greek, the Septuagint. Moreover, philosophy had passed its heyday, pagan religions never quite seemed to deliver and the human heart seemed to cry out for answers and the Answer. On the other hand, there was a much darker side to the world: military might and brutality, as the Romans tolerated no rivals; economic exploitation epitomised by slavery; sexual immorality on an unimaginable scale.

How you read 'when the time had fully come' will reflect your view of God. Was it that the Lord thought 'Aha, this looks as good a time as any!' so we have a God who reacts to human history? Or, rather, was it this point in history that God had prepared way ahead of time? Either way, do not ignore the huge implication. Christianity is to do with an historical faith, 'it happened in time' faith. So when other faiths come along centuries later that purport to improve or supersede Christianity, here's the answer: we cannot re-write history like that. Why? Because of this momentous event, 'God sent his Son' (v4).

The One we know as Jesus not only existed before his coming, like an angel might. He existed before as the eternal Son. The Son is no afterthought. He is God's prime thought, the eternal Word, who was in the beginning with God (Jn. 1:1,2). It was this Son, the delight of heaven, whom the Father 'sent', literally 'apostled out' into the world. How did he arrive? 'Born of a woman.'

Many years ago, I had various discussions with a man who believed that Jesus was an astronaut! What eventually convinced him of the truth of the Christian faith and the absurdity of his belief was what we call the Virgin Birth. When the Son of God entered the human race, the incarnation, he did not do a 'Beam me down, Scotty.' He became a foetus in a virgin's womb, a baby in her arms, a child at her knee, a youth who learned a trade at his father's side, a man about town. Yet he never ceased to be what he was and ever will be, the Son of God, whose hands had 'flung stars into space.' Moreover, he was 'under law', circumcised the eighth day, taking his responsibilities to the law personally when he underwent his bar mitzvah before his teens, and making it his custom to be in synagogue on the Sabbath (Lk. 2:21-53; 4:16). Why? To redeem us. Here's the astonishing historical claim of the Christian faith. God became one of us to do what the name Jesus means: to be 'God the Saviour/Rescuer.' All the human race is 'under law' and bondage of one type or another. In Jesus Christ, God takes law's curse, judgment and death and makes our doom his own.

In the recent series of *24*, Jack Bauer, a counter-terrorist agent, has been left to die in a Chinese prison by the American administration. However, a terrorist promises an end to the wave of suicide bombings on the streets of the USA if America procures Bauer's release. Upon his release, however, he is to be handed over to the terrorist to avenge the death of his brother who died at Bauer's hands. So Bauer is released from his Chinese prison, brought to the USA and then told he is to be handed over to die at the hands of this terrorist for the nation's peace. He accepts, with words to the effect, 'I would rather die for something than dying for nothing in that Chinese prison.' Fascinating fiction! Enter, gospel truth: Christ died for somethings and someones 'that we might receive the full rights of sons' (v5). The latter phrase means 'place into the condition of a son' or 'adopt.'

In the world of Paul's day, adoption meant at least three things: a new legal standing, a new name and a new relationship. In Jesus Christ, I have a new standing with God – I'm justified. I bear a new name, Christian. I have a new family, God for my Father and every Christian as my brother or sister. But that is not all the good news. Occasionally, I have met children who were adopted by their parents at a very young age and I have noted something astonishing: their mannerisms, speech, even their looks would suggest they were natural born children. They have taken on the family resemblance. That is why verse 6 is so exciting, because a Christian is not only 'legally adopted' but someone who is being morally and spiritually transformed into the family likeness. How? By God sending 'the Spirit of his Son into our hearts' (v6), so that Christ is formed in us (19 and see Romans 8:29). How do we know? Here is one of the major strands of Christian assurance: 'the Spirit who calls out, "Abba, Father."' 'Abba' is language used for intimacy and trust within a family and is found on our Lord's own lips in prayer (Mk. 14:36). Slaves were expressly forbidden to use it of their master. But now in Christ we discover that we have a new master who is our Father, the God of the whole universe is our 'Dad.' Elsewhere we are told that, 'The Spirit himself testifies with our spirit that we are God's children' (Rom. 8:16).

In C.S. Lewis's *The Lion, the Witch and the Wardrobe*, the fawn, Mr Tumnus, tells Lucy that Narnia is a place where 'It's always winter, but never Christmas' because of the evil witch. Satan would rob the world, and every Christian if he could, of the astonishing experience of being 'no longer a slave, but a son . . . an heir' (v7). So we do not need to stay a 'nipper' in winterland. Because of Christ's 'Christmas'– his first coming, his 'Easter'– his death, his 'Pentecost'– his coming by the Spirit, we can cry out '*Abba*, Father.' Let's do so.

● *What are the traces of family likeness that we should expect to see increasingly in ourselves and others after conversion? How can we encourage them?*

SO, WHERE ARE YOU OFF TO?

'So where are you off to?' How many times I asked that
question of my then teenagers when I was not at all sure of
the wisdom of where and with whom they were going. In
the light of the previous sections, it is precisely what Paul
fears: 'Do you wish to be enslaved . . . again?' (v9). Since
Jesus has brought us into God's family, it is the height of
folly, says Paul, to return to slavery. Since the Triune God
had rescued them (note the Trinitarian structure of verses
4-7: God, Son, Spirit), how could they return to 'weak and
miserable principles' (v9)? In verse 3, 'principles' seemed
to indicate basic moral teaching: here it has a far darker
meaning, for it is related to 'those who by nature are not
gods' (v8). These 'principles', originally the four traditional
elements of 'earth, wind, fire and water', became associated
with the signs of the zodiac and the belief that various spirits
controlled heavenly bodies and the destinies of people. It
was a form of astrology. We have not advanced much since
Paul's day. For instance, recently I saw the late, lamented
Princess Diana's personal astrologer being interviewed on
TV. Likewise, daily newspapers carry horoscopes.

In Galatians, these 'weak and miserable principles'
exerted their influence on these believers in the form of
'observing special days and months and seasons and years'
(v10), the repeated 'and' deliberately echoing the drudgery
and repetitious nonsense of it all (try reading the phrase
out loud, emphasising the 'and' – you'll get the idea). For a
period in the 1990s, anyone connected to management
development might well have found themselves on a
course where yogic techniques for meditation, under the
guise of personal development, were being taught. You
might be wise to check out whether some visualisation
methods are being taught in your child's school. So much
for twenty-first century technology and sophistication!

For Paul, however, as for any Christian leader, the depressing thing was not that such 'principles'– or 'principalities and powers' (Eph. 6:10-18) – existed, but that 'sons of God' should be drawn back to them. Little wonder he feared he may have wasted his efforts on them (v11).

A slave or a son is the stark choice in this passage. Before his conversion to Christ, John Wesley was an ordained minister of the Church of England and a would-be missionary to American Indians. During his voyage to the States, he discovered that he had only 'the faith of a slave.' After his conversion, on 24th May 1738 in Aldersgate Street, London, he spoke of his heart 'being strangely warmed' towards Christ and an assurance being given him that he was a child of God. A real, vibrant Christian faith must not descend into mere duty, drudgery and demand, 'basic principles' (v3). If it does, for some it may lead still further to 'weak and miserable principles' of the 'dark lord' instead of Jesus the Lord of light. Don't be a 'nipper', don't stay a slave. Live as a son and heir of your Abba Father.

FURTHER STUDY
Read Romans 8:15-17. 'The Spirit himself testifies with our spirit that we are God's children' (v.16). How might we recognise this 'testifying with our spirit' that we are indeed co-heirs with Christ?

REFLECTION AND RESPONSE
- Corrie Ten Boom used to carry around with her a piece of embroidery with a cross stitched on the front. On the back were all knotted and tangled threads. Sometimes our lives look like the back of that embroidery – but in reality, we are sons and daughters of God, with a great inheritance. Praise God that you are a joint-heir with Christ today!

- Do you find it hard to call God 'Father'? Because of imperfect relationships, many people struggle with the concept of God as their heavenly 'Dad.' Our experiences with our own fathers can colour the way we perceive our heavenly Father. Ask the Spirit of God to reveal God to you as Father.

SMALL GROUP DISCUSSION POINT
All together, read the Lord's Prayer. Note that it begins 'Our Father.' How can we better support each other as brothers and sisters in Christ when we face temptation to return to a previous lifestyle, or are tempted to give up when the going gets tough?

CHAPTER 13

Love your local leader

GALATIANS 4:12-20

Aim: To examine our attitudes towards leadership

FOCUS ON THE THEME:
Mrs Perkins saw Mrs West in the supermarket and wondered how the new minister in Mrs West's church was settling in. 'Oh, no one likes him,' said the friend, dismissively. 'Why not?' asked Mrs Perkins, surprised. 'Well, Pastor Frank used to stand by the door and shake hands with everyone. He visited old Betty twice a week and this new man doesn't. *And* the new man's changed the chairs – we're all facing the window now.' Mrs West shook her head. 'No one likes him. Betty's not coming to church any more. I might leave, too. . . unless he puts those chairs back as they should be.' How should we treat our leaders? Why do people get hung up on petty issues?

Reading: Galatians 4:12-20
Key verses: Galatians 4:19,20

'Steve, I just burned out; don't let it happen to you!' This was wise advice from an older pastor to me in my early days of ministry. Recently, in a local supermarket, I met another casualty, equally burned out and disillusioned by pastoral ministry. The statistics on leaders who have 'lost it' because of overwork, moral indiscretion, financial hardship or whatever, make depressing reading. Burn-out is no respecter of denominational affiliation: angry Anglicans, beaten-up Baptists, cheesed off Charismatics – try the rest of the alphabet for yourself. Somewhere along the way, a crack has become a chasm between a group of Christians and their leader(s).

In Paul's words to these Galatians, we detect the apostle's pastoral heart. If the first three chapters portray him as the theologian, apologist, missionary-statesman and lawyer, here is Paul the pastor-preacher massively concerned for the well-being of his flock, his 'brothers' (v12) and 'dear children' (v19) in the faith. There are principles here that any leader and every local church neglect at their peril.

IT ISN'T WRONG TO ESTEEM GOOD LEADERS

What is evident in these verses is the esteem these Galatians had for Paul, their founding apostle. How come Paul came to Galatia in the first place? Was it blinding revelation, a 'Macedonian call' (Acts 16:9,10)? Hardly – 'it was because of an illness' (v13). Galatia had not been on Paul's itinerary, but it was on God's. As to the nature of his illness, we can only speculate (ophthalmia, malaria, epilepsy have all been suggested). But that illness got him to Galatia and he 'preached the gospel' to them (v13). Let everyone who believes that perfect health is a Christian's right and God's will *now*, if one only has faith, ponder these phrases 'an illness . . . my illness' (13,14).

When my wife, Brenda, was first diagnosed with multiple sclerosis in 1979, we thought the sky had fallen in. However, in a very short time, we began to meet others who had the same condition, including Jacqui, a twenty-eight year old graphic artist. Her type of MS was the most virulent and she was early confined to a wheelchair. But over a period of months, she came to Christ and I buried that lovely young woman 'in sure and certain hope of the resurrection to eternal life.' Brenda's illness gave the opportunity to preach the gospel to her. How amazing are God's sovereign purposes of grace.

In the Greco-Roman and Jewish worlds, physical deformity or illness was viewed as a sign of divine displeasure (Jn. 9:2). Whatever the nature of Paul's illness, however much it 'was a trial' (v14), the Galatians did not let it get in the way. They treated Paul as royalty: 'you welcomed me . . . as if I were Christ Jesus himself' (v14). Like the Thessalonians before them, they 'welcomed the message' and the messenger 'with joy' (1 Thes. 1:6). He was treated with neither 'contempt nor scorn' (v14), an alliterated phrase in Greek. So we might translate as 'you neither ridiculed nor rejected me . . . neither despised nor derided me.' Rather, they received him as if he were the Lord Jesus himself. Why?

I suspect that it had something to do with Paul's manner and demeanour. I recently conducted a friend's funeral, attended by many non-Christians. It had been a very moving, Christ-centred service. A fine, godly older lady shook my hand as she was leaving the service. 'Steve, it's not what we say but also the way we say it, isn't it?' I replied with an instant 'Yes, it is!' and then was left to ponder, 'Did I "tell it like it is" or tell it like Jesus?' Paul says 'I became like you' (v12), which means that his approach to them was one of getting alongside where they were: 'to those not having the law I became like one not having the law . . . for the sake of the gospel' (1 Cor. 9:21,23). When Gladys Aylward was asked about the secret of her 'success' in China, she replied, 'It was simple, I became one of them!' Paul had learned that secret from the God who had likewise changed addresses and became one of us (v4, Jn. 1:14). But there's a further stage. Paul adds – 'become like me' (v12).

I imagine few of us feel comfortable, as leaders, to ask people to 'become like me.' 'No! Be like Jesus!' we'd want to say. Elsewhere, Paul urges believers to follow his example, 'as I follow the example of Christ' (1 Cor. 11:1). In other words, to some degree, Christian leaders need to embody what they preach. In context, the phrase may mean no more than – don't fall back into legalism but stay, like I do, a free man in Jesus. Whatever, leaders must model their teaching if it is to be effective.

In addition, Paul pleads for (v12) a return to the 'good old days.' When he first came, they would gladly 'have torn out your eyes and given them to me', such was their 'joy' (v15) at receiving the gospel. His reason for this reminder is part of the larger concern he has that his converts don't defect from the gospel. I remember years ago, a lady, a young Christian, was on the point of leaving the church and joining a cult. It was this taking her back to 'all your joy' (v15) that God used to keep her going on with Christ.

We may not be able to think of our leaders as 'an angel of God' (v14). That's a big ask for most Christians I know! But love, affection, esteem and support are so right for leaders who are gospel men and women. Like Paul, they may have an illness, or not be particularly outwardly attractive, or the most bubbly personality in town. However, the real question is, do they 'preach the gospel' (v13) even when it hurts? Let me be more specific.

What could you do to encourage your leadership this week? One of my favourite leadership illustrations is drawn from sandhill cranes, birds who migrate vast distances together, flying in a 'V' flock formation. Apparently, such a formation provides 73% more aerodynamic uplift for them. These 'smart' birds arrange themselves so that the strongest birds are in front at the point of the 'V', where most of the turbulence is. In addition, they regularly rotate the leadership so no bird gets burned out. As they are flying, all the other birds are 'honking' their approval to the leaders. In whatever way is appropriate, express your appreciation to those in leadership who are 'telling you the truth' (v16). By 'honking' your approval, you may find they perform better than ever. Do you know anyone who died from too much encouragement?

● *Pray for your leaders to increasingly model Jesus. What could you do to encourage them this week?*

IT IS WRONG TO TOLERATE FALSE TEACHERS

The problem in Galatia was not that they esteemed leaders. The real danger was they would esteem the wrong ones, the false teachers. Three times Paul uses 'zealous' in two verses (vs 17,18). 'Zealous' carries the idea of being devoted to, being passionate about something, to the point where flattery, jealousy, envy and spite may kick in. The agenda of Paul's opponents was clear: 'to win you over' and simultaneously 'alienate you from us' (v17). There is nothing new about spiritual empire building. Does this mean that mega-churches, with mega-money and mega-preaching 'stars', must be wrong? No. 'It is fine to be zealous, provided the purpose is good' (v18).

When I was a pastor of one of the largest churches in my town, although we were net exporters of members to other churches, still the myth persisted that we were empire building by luring people from other churches to our preaching centre. It gave me great joy to welcome people who had found Christ in spite of their pagan or cult affiliation. It was always a lesser joy to act as a life-boat for believers from churches that had hit the rocks or were going round in circles. Empire building? The only 'empire' our

church leadership was interested in was that of Emperor
Jesus, and winning the lost for him.

In Galatia it was different. A read of the Acts of the
Apostles quickly confirms how much Paul's gospel
ministry was hounded by his opponents (for example, Acts
14:1-20). By flattery, innuendo and deception, these false
teachers aimed to uncouple the Galatian believers from
Paul – 'to alienate you'– then attach those so deceived to
themselves – 'zealous for them' (v17). But the result of that
process, ultimately, would be to detach these believers from
the gospel and therefore from Christ.

False teachers do not only work outside of the local
church. When they infiltrate our ranks (2:4), they develop
what has been called an 'Absalom spirit.' Do you remember
him? He was king David's good-looking son who, by
flattery, 'stole the hearts of the men of Israel' (2 Sam. 15:6.
You can get the bigger story by reading through chapters
15-19). The result of his rebellion was that the people of
God no longer followed the Lord's anointed, the king.
Similarly, Paul had warned the Ephesian elders that after
his departure 'savage wolves will come in among you and
will not spare the flock. Even from your own number men
will arise and distort the truth in order to draw disciples
after them.' The same was happening in Galatia, and this
pastoral appeal functions in the same way as his warning to
the Ephesian elders: 'So be on your guard!' (Acts 20:29-31).

Such warnings to hold on to the apostolic gospel are as
pertinent to twenty-first century church as the first century
church. One of the Anglican traditions I enjoy is the phrase
used after the public reading of Scripture: 'This is the word
of the Lord', to which the congregation responds, 'Thanks
be to God!' In one Anglican church, this form of words and
response had been previously glued to the lectern but
removed. When a new minister asked why, a church
warden told him that the previous vicar had insisted on its

removal. He no longer believed the Bible to be the word of the Lord. 'If anyone is ashamed of me and my words . . . the Son of Man will be ashamed of him', warns the Lord Jesus (Mk. 8:38). On the Day of Judgment, I know whose approval alone I will cherish.

If the foregoing seems harsh, remember true pastors must be tied to truth telling (v16), however costly or uncomfortable that is. Such faithfulness may cost a preacher preferment, payment, imprisonment or even death. On one occasion, Abraham Lincoln gave an unpopular speech to the Senate. His response to criticism is wonderful: 'If it is deemed I should go down because of this speech, let me go down nailed to truth.' He did not go down: two years later he became President of the United States. A day will come when faithful leaders will likewise shine in glory.

So, here's a good general test of someone's teaching. Does it always pump you up, make you feel good about yourself and the speaker? Or are there times when the truth has hurt you, when you have been stung and your conscience stabbed awake? Faithful teachers and leaders, like good preaching, learn how to comfort the disturbed and disturb the comfortable. False teachers merely stroke egos. Be careful of those who want 'to win you over, but for no good' (v17).

● *If we start to doubt that the Bible is the word of God, what effect will this have on our relationship with Jesus, with other believers and our effectiveness in sharing the gospel?*

IT'S ALWAYS RIGHT TO STAY WITH THE TRUTH

Elsewhere, in his letter, Paul can speak like a 'father' to his converts (1 Cor. 4:15) or 'a mother caring for her little children' (1 Thes. 2:7). Any day soon, as I write, my daughter will be 'in the pains of childbirth' (v19) with our third grandchild. She cannot wait for the 'bump', as the babe is affectionately known, to arrive and to be free of the daily discomfort she has experienced during her pregnancy. Yet Paul uses the word 'again' as if he is having to undergo all the spiritual birth pangs he felt when these Galatians came to Christ. It's as if they were being 'born again' again! In reality, what he longed for is what every pastor desires for the church, that 'Christ . . . is formed in you' (v19), so that we 'take the shape of Christ' (NEB). Becoming a spiritual babe is one thing, becoming a mature Christian is another. Yet Christ-likeness is one of the major goals of conversion (Col. 1:28).

Paul's pastoral instinct and desire was to be there personally with these believers (v20). Why? Many of us know the problems of writing a letter. A letter can't smile. You cannot always pick up the nuances. You may take something seriously that was said in jest. Face to face encounters, especially pastorally (and often in business), can do the trick where a 'phone call, email or letter cannot. Paul could not be with them, but it did not stop his pastoral heart beating for them: 'I am perplexed about you' (v20), or ' at my wit's end' (JBP), says Paul. How does your leader feel about you – 'joy' (v15) or 'perplexity' (v20)?

In summary, here are some mutual obligations for pastoral leaders and their flocks. For 'sheep', if your leaders faithfully 'tell you the truth' (v16) from the word of God, then you need to 'hold them in the highest regard in love because of their work' (1 Thes. 5:13). They deserve your respect, loyalty, affection, prayers and, if necessary, your financial support (more on that when we come to 6:6). It is an old but too near the truth joke that many Christians have two 'roasts' for Sunday – roast beef and roast preacher!

For those in leadership in the local church, it is essential that they bear people on their hearts, and long for Christ to be 'formed in you' (v19). It was said of one Professor of Philosophy, in his *Times* obituary, that, at the end of the day, he was more in love with ideas than he was with people. I have come across some leaders and have wondered if they received their training in pastoral skills from some SS Commandant. 'A hired hand . . . cares nothing for the sheep' (Jn. 10:10-13), Jesus tells us. The Lord's people matter to the Lord and to any true pastor. Do they matter to you?

FURTHER STUDY

It is well worth taking some time to look through the books in the New Testament, to see what is said about those who would be leaders (e.g. 1 Thess. 5:12,13; 1 Tim. 3:1-12, 5:17-20; 2 Tim.2:14-26; Titus 1:5-9).

REFLECTION AND RESPONSE

- Think about the Focus on the Theme. Hopefully, you support your leader more than this lady did! It is good to give loyalty and support to a leader, but it is also right to challenge those who we can see are not acting in accordance with the word of God. We should be able to query leaders' actions. Having said that, leadership is not for the faint-hearted! Think about what constitutes a healthy and balanced attitude to the leadership within your own church.

- Spend some time praying for specific leaders in your fellowship. If any needs are known to you, bring them before the Lord. Think of ways to encourage those leading Sunday school, running Mums and Toddlers or Senior Citizens events or involved in youth work.

SMALL GROUP DISCUSSION POINT

We have spent time before thinking about ways to encourage leaders. Spend some time in prayer for your leaders now. Make sure people feel safe to share anything that is worrying or troubling them in regards to leadership issues. How can you show your leaders how grateful you are to them – would it be possible to arrange a special meal at someone's home?

CHAPTER 14

A tale of two cities

GALATIANS 4:21-31

Aim: To think about the spiritual nature of sonship in the kingdom of God

---

FOCUS ON THE THEME:
There you are, with your holiday luggage, standing at the foot of the mountain staring up at the sheer face. On the top of the mountain is a beautiful hotel. You've got a choice. You can either try to climb up yourself (impossible!), or you can wait for the funicular railway. Not rocket science, is it? Why then do so many of us try to climb up the impossible cliff face to a kingdom we can never reach – on our own?

Reading: Galatians 4:21-31
Key verse: Galatians 4:28

Our title echoes Charles Dickens's memorable novel, set during the French Revolution. It also introduces us to another revolution involving two cities which bear the same name: Jerusalem, 'the present city' (v25) and one 'that is above' (v26). At first reading, Paul's sentiments about the Galatians – 'I am perplexed about you' (v20) – may well be our reaction to this complex passage. It is full of historical allusions, theological inferences and spiritual applications that may appear both mysterious and even arbitrary. In actual fact, its main point and purpose become clear: 'we are not children of the slave woman, but of the free woman' (v31). In other words, the major theme of slavery versus liberty is still in Paul's mind so he continues to argue his case by changing tactics from the personal and pastoral approach of the previous section (v12-20) to what may be called a more rabbinical style of argumentation aimed directly at those 'who want to be under the law' (v21).

It is both instructive and wise to note Paul's method here. These Galatian Christians were impressed by the seeming grasp of the law that Paul's opponents displayed. So he decides to take the opposition on in their own back yard, so to speak. Or, in football terms, he is going to play this important FA cup tie 'away' on their ground. He will use their presuppositions, their arguments, their starting points against them, as one might use an opponent's body weight against him as in a martial art like judo. His method is a variety of what we call apologetics. That is not apologising for our faith but defending it, showing why there are very good reasons to believe. In our increasingly secular, post-Christian world we need to know not only what we believe and why but what others believe too.

At one level, apologetics is a rubble clearing exercise. We are seeking to deal with objections to the Christian faith that swirl around in people's minds. Take George, a firm believer in God but not at all sure where or why Jesus fitted in. After weeks and weeks of meeting up, debating this or that, he looked me straight in the eye one day: 'Steve, what are you going to say to God if, on judgement day, he asks you why you believed in Jesus rather than simply in him?' I took a deep breath and replied, 'Well, I'll say, "Lord, it's your fault! Because if Jesus isn't who he claimed to be, you should never have raised him from the dead!"' He sat there stunned for a little while then, pointing to his head, he said 'I think my problem isn't here any more but,' pointing to his heart, 'here!' He came to Christ that afternoon. 'We demolish arguments and every pretension that sets itself up against the knowledge of God', says Paul elsewhere (2 Cor. 10:5). For one or two of my readers, this 'apologetic ministry' may be your life's calling. You may learn how to help doubters of the gospel to doubt their doubts and come to faith, reasoning people out of their unreasonable unbelief. It is amazing how much faith one needs to be a full-blown and consistent atheist these days!

- *'All roads lead to heaven. The God of the Christian is the same as the God of the Hindu. Jesus was just a prophet, like Mohammed'? How would you answer this person?*

Coming directly to the passage itself, we will divide it into three bite-size chunks – the historical, figurative and spiritual.

SETTING THE SCENE HISTORICALLY

Once again, Paul goes to Genesis and Abraham, and presupposes that his readers are familiar with chapters 12-21. In outline, here are the relevant events. Abram left Ur of the Chaldees childless but with a promise of a family (Gen. 12:1-4). A decade passed and nothing happened. So Sarai took providence into her own hands and Abram, at her instigation, slept with Hagar her maid, who fell pregnant and made Abram a father at eighty-six (Gen. 16:16). But there was to be no domestic bliss in this home. Whether it is the ancient or modern world, three's a crowd. Hagar began to despise her mistress, an understandable reaction by anyone who has ever been used sexually, whatever that society's cultural mores may be. A 'bust-up' was inevitable but, at God's intervention, the runaway Hagar returned (Gen. 16:6-15). Over a dozen years elapsed and still no son of promise had appeared. At ninety-nine, Abram must have concluded that was that:

perhaps Ishmael should be the chosen one (17:18). But, no, for the Lord appeared, re-emphasised his promise, and changed their names to Abraham and Sarah respectively. Further assurance was given to them that a boy was on the way, Isaac by name (check out Genesis 17). Sure enough, one year later 'at the very time God had promised him', Isaac arrived, born to parents one hundred and ninety years old respectively (Gen. 17:17). Peace reigned for about three years, but one day Sarah concluded that Ishmael's relationship to his kid brother, whom he had been mocking, was a threat to her son. The result? Hagar and Ishmael were driven away, never to return to the family, save for Abraham's funeral (Gen. 25:9). As Paul summarises the situation, one son 'was born in the ordinary way', the other 'as the result of a promise' (v23). One birth was natural, the other supernatural. The writer to the Hebrews tells us that this latter birth was directly linked to faith. 'By faith Abraham, even though he was past age – and Sarah herself was barren – was enabled to become a father because he considered him faithful who had made the promise' (Heb. 11:11).

● *Is there some specific promise you believe God has made to you? Have you checked it out with others as being biblical? Are you wondering whether God can be trusted? 'Consider him faithful': your 'Isaac's' arrival may be nearer than you think.*

So much for the scene-setting. Paul says there is another way of reading these historical events.

INTERPRETING THE STORY FIGURATIVELY

Paul's interpretation of these historical events was both necessary and dangerous: necessary for him, dangerous for us. To the rabbinical mind of his day, the literal or historical level of meaning was not exhaustive. Other levels, the 'figurative' included (v24), could be discerned. So Paul's method here was both necessary and brilliant. Separated by two thousand years from him, it is dangerous to assume that we can do likewise without specific biblical warrant. Otherwise, it is altogether possible to spiritualise the literal or to literalise the spiritual and make the Bible mean anything except what it says. Two illustrations must suffice. For instance, on the one hand, someone may say, 'What the resurrection of Jesus *really* means is that somehow new life is possible after tragedy, for of course Jesus didn't physically rise from the dead!' On the other hand, another states that phrases like 'the hand of God', 'the eyes of the Lord' etc are not figurative but literal; so God is really a 'Big Man' up in the sky with a body, arms, legs etc. If you have been around a certain type of church, you will have your own list of hilarious horror stories and lessons on how not to handle Scripture. The key phrase about the figurative is 'proceed with caution.'

This history of Abraham was 'spoken with another meaning in mind' (v24 JBP), the underlying Greek word giving us the English 'allegory.' Sarah and Hagar represent two covenants. One is based on the promise of grace in which God says, 'I will, I will', the other on law which says, 'You do, you do' (3:8,12). Let's look more closely at the contrasts.

Hagar was Abraham's 'second wife', not his first, Sarah, to whom the promises were made. Likewise, law came '430 years later' (3:17) after what 'God in his grace gave' to Abraham (3:18). Moreover, Hagar and her son were slaves, a note sounded repeatedly in this passage (at least seven times). But Sarah was a 'free woman' and her son was 'born as a result of the promise' (v23). The point is that Hagar was never meant to be the bearer of miraculous life, just as the law could not impart it (3:21). All the latter could do, like Hagar, was to produce children 'in the ordinary way' (v23), since 'flesh gives birth to flesh', according to Jesus (Jn. 3:6). According to Genesis, Ishmael was a wild donkey of a man, whose hand was against everyone (Gen. 16:12). He graphically illustrates human nature. It is wild and potentially untameable (Gal. 5:17). Legislation, of course, whether biblical or secular, may curb, correct and help civilise people. At one level, we ought to be profoundly grateful for it. However, it has its limits, as Martin Luther King knew in his fight for racial justice: 'Morality cannot be legislated, but behaviour may be regulated. Judicial decrees may not change hearts, but they can restrict the heartless.'[4]

'Judicial decrees may not change the heart' is the issue here. Law operates on the horizontal plane, even though it may be from a 'Mount Sinai in Arabia' (v25), where the law was given. Sinai's terrain was rugged, bleak, barren and unforgiving. Life without the grace of God can be just that, a desolate wilderness. Indeed, not just life generally but religion in particular is in view here, 'the present city of Jerusalem . . . in slavery with her children' (v25). Out of context, this may sound anti-Semitic. Remember, however, that it was written by a very Jewish Jew who loved his own people deeply (Rom. 9:1-5). Paul knows, of course, all about Judaism's high moral and ethical standards, and the rules that covered life from the cradle to the grave. Moreover, Judaism was not monochrome. There were major differences between, for instance, the Sadducees and the Pharisees and then further sub-divisions within their ranks. What is common and well-documented, however, is the passion and commitment of many first century Jews to their religion. It is paralleled by similar zeal and dedication found in hundreds of twenty-first century religions. Very often, their devotees' enthusiasm and sacrifice are a challenge and rebuke to comfortable and costless Christianity.

Astonishingly, religion may be pervasive and all-consuming and still be explained as 'born in the ordinary way' (v23), in other words, natural. The Gospels and Acts are a record of many self-righteous Jews opposing the gospel, though that is not the whole picture: thousands of other Jews came to believe that, in Jesus, the Messiah had come and a new age begun. In Christ, life was no longer lived on the merely horizontal plane. God had intervened vertically and they had been 'born by the power of the Spirit' (v29) or 'from above' (Jn. 3:3 margin: NIV). Their new centre of gravity had therefore become the 'Jerusalem that is above' (v26). Rightly understood, this is what the Old Testament was always looking forward toward – its fulfilment in Jesus Christ. Not everyone, then and now, agreed.

Let's pull these strands together a little more tightly. Like Sarah, the first wife, grace precedes law, just as Abraham is prior to Moses, and God's promise predates human performance. It is God's grace that bestows spiritual life supernaturally. It is not bestowed 'in the ordinary way' (v23). Such grace makes its recipients sons of the free and children of God. In so doing, the believer's true spiritual location is no longer earthly but heavenly, 'the Jerusalem above' (v26). Elsewhere we are told that this city 'is coming down out of heaven' from God (Rev. 3:12). So here and now Christians discover that their ultimate reference point is not a location on an earthly map but a citizenship in heaven (Phil. 3:20).

The foregoing has massive implications for both time and eternity. Although it would be folly to underestimate our backgrounds and ethnicity, it is tragic when Christians define themselves by where they come from, whom they know, which church they belong to, etc. Religion without Christ provides all of that and more. To be 'all one in Christ Jesus' (3:28), however, depends on a shared experience of new birth. Accordingly, we need a radical paradigm shift in our thinking that defines us as the people of God linked to *history* via Abraham, to God's new *family*, the Church, via grace, and to *eternity* via God's promise.

To put it as simply as I can, if we are to be members of God's kingdom, we must be supernaturally changed. That is why Paul's quotation from Isaiah 54:1 in verse 27 is so telling. It was written to a people in Babylonian captivity who despaired of freedom and the future of their race. But the Lord assures them of divine intervention. All they needed was . . . a miracle! For the Church of Jesus to multiply depends on the power of God. I recall an old preacher talking about the difference between a brick and a stone in connection with the growth of the Church. The former, he pointed out, was humanly manufactured. It is what religion, Christian or otherwise, may produce: bricks that all look pretty much the same. In contrast, stones are all sorts of different shapes and sizes, each unique. When Jesus promises to 'build my church' (Mt. 16:18), his materials are not 'bricks', humanly manufactured entities. Rather, they are 'stones', indeed 'living stones' (1 Pet. 2:5), supernaturally created. Religion can only produce children 'in slavery.' The gospel produces children 'born as the result of a promise' (v23). To be part of God's family a spiritual transformation is required.

- 'We don't want you becoming a religious nut! And we don't want you preaching at us, either!' Words from a church-goer to her newly born-again grandchild. How would you counsel anyone who is experiencing opposition to their faith by their own 'religious' family members?

- A cul-de-sac ending in a brick wall. . . a skylark soaring in the sky. How do these two images illustrate the difference between 'religion' and spiritual transformation?

UNDERSTANDING SONSHIP SPIRITUALITY

To be a child of God is simultaneously an invitation to privilege and a call to responsibility. In terms of privilege, the believer is 'born by the power of the Spirit' (v29). The Christian is now 'the free woman's son' (v30), and belongs to the Jerusalem above (v26), and his name is written in heaven (Heb. 12:23). The result is that we now have an 'inheritance' (v30) – we are 'heirs according to the promise' (3:29 and 4:7). In fact, we are 'co-heirs with Christ' (Rom. 8:17) – a prospect so staggering as to be beyond imagination.

In terms of responsibility, the flip side to our privileges is persecution, which is how Paul describes the events recorded in Genesis 21:9 where Ishmael ridiculed young Isaac. 'It is the same now', he adds (v29). In the first centuries of the Church, Rome, with all its imperial might, persecuted Christians; in the twentieth century, both Fascism and Marxism have done the same. None of this is surprising, since totalitarian claims of 'Caesar is Lord', in the first or twentieth century, are resisted by the Bible's insistence that 'Jesus is Lord.' But some of the most virulent opposition to Christian faith throughout two thousand years has come from an unexpected source, religion itself. One only needs to read of the riots, stonings and imprisonments that the Book of Acts records, or to take a cursory glance at the world today where totalitarian religious systems function, to see the truth of the principle of persecution being illustrated. A little while ago, I sat in a room with a group of Iranian young people, three of whose fathers had been martyred for no other crime than following Christ.

But let's bring the issues nearer home. There are churches and denominations who appear to loathe the very gospel they are supposed to proclaim. Some of my ministerial colleagues have had very rough rides in churches that have become congregations of the self-righteous, in which leaders who have been 'born in the ordinary way' resist those 'born by the power of the Spirit.' I think it was the American satirist Lenny Bruce who said, 'Everyday people are leaving the Church and finding God.' Tragic but true! And still nearer home – ensure that your religion does not get between you and the Lord Jesus! To all false religion, God says 'Get rid of the slave woman and her son' for there's no 'inheritance' to be found there (v30).

Dickens's *A Tale of Two Cities* ends dramatically with Sidney Carton willingly going to La Guillotine in another's place: Charles Darnay walks free from prison and into life. The book's final sentence records Carton's words: 'It is a far, far better thing that I do, than I have ever done; it is a far, far better rest that I go to than I have ever known.' Another has willingly sacrificed himself for us so we may escape and walk free in life. You may wish to appropriate Carton's words for yourself. There is a 'better rest' offered to us in Jesus – 'Come . . . I will give you rest' (Mt. 11:28). For 'the far better thing' has been done for us by Christ – he 'gave himself' for us (2:20). Those who rely on him alone are 'born by the power of the Spirit' (v29), children of promise and inheritors of the Kingdom. Rejoice!

FURTHER STUDY

Read Jesus' words about the Holy Spirit in John 3. Note especially verse 8, and spend some moments thinking about the power and the mystery of the Spirit of God.

REFLECTION AND RESPONSE

- Reflect on the awesome power of the Spirit to change our hearts and our lives.

- Thank God for any changes you can see in people who have stopped 'working' and started 'resting' in him.

- Sidney Carton gave everything he had for one he loved, but up until that time he had lived a wasted life. Jesus had not! He laid aside his majesty to come to the earth for you and for me (Phil. 2:6-11). Reflect on what Jesus gave up to come to earth, and thank him for it.

SMALL GROUP DISCUSSION POINT

Think of reasons people might resist the work of the Spirit of God in their lives (e.g. fear, lack of understanding, spiritual blindness). Make sure everyone knows this is a safe place to share their own doubts and fears. Pray for one another to be open to the work of the Holy Spirit in your individual lives – and in the life of your church; changing, healing, restoring, setting you free from works so you can truly experience the true rest of spiritual sonship.

CHAPTER 15

Born free

GALATIANS 5:1-12

Aim: To challenge us to walk in the freedom Christ has bought for us

---

FOCUS ON THE THEME:
'I choose God! . . . And what now, friend?' . . . 'Well, there's a Bible study on Monday, the church meeting's Wednesday evening, Thursday there's a nurture group . . . Friday night there's a coach going to see John Wimber, Saturday there's a day-long conference on next year's mission, and Sunday it's service in the morning, Azerbaijanian meal at lunchtime, and communion in the evening.' . . . 'Free at last!'[5]

Reading: Galatians 5:1-12
Key verse: Galatians 5:1

It was September 1978 when I actually saw, in the flesh, this stunning lady, a film star with an international reputation. Before then, I had only seen her on film. She had been one of the world's great free spirits, but not any more. She was an older lady and now behind bars, imprisoned in Gerald Durrell's zoo in Jersey, Channel Isles. Elsa the lioness (actually a stand-in for the original Elsa who died aged five in 1961) had been the star of the 1966 film, *Born Free*; born free but spending her last days as a captive.

'It is for freedom that Christ has set us free' (v1) Paul declares. Yet he is painfully aware that it is one thing to be 'born free' and another to 'live free.' The danger these Christians faced was their lurch into legalism, 'a yoke of slavery' (v1) when the Liberator had come 'to release the oppressed' (Lk. 4:18). Legalism is a great thief; it steals from us the joy of salvation and sucks from us the lifeblood of grace. It makes the Christian life merely Christian liability to obey the whole law (v3). And the really depressing element of legalism is that it can appear so attractive, not merely to the lackadaisical Christian but, more subtly, to the really committed one. Legalism promises 'more', but, in actual fact, always delivers less because ultimately it alienates us from Christ (v4). Remember, legalism is not to be confused with living a disciplined, Christ-centred life ('the life I live in the body. I live by faith in the Son of God', 2:20). Legalism is the notion that my actions, my good, my 'doing my bit' somehow or other contribute towards, earn and merit salvation and lead to successful Christian living. It often expresses itself by that self-righteous smugness that arises from believing we have ticked all the right boxes and declare ourselves 'OK.'

So does it not matter how we live? It is really a question of motivation. Why do I do what I do? Is it because of the 'Son of God who loved me . . . and gave himself for me' (2:20)? If so, that is gratitude, a 'faith expressing itself through love' (v6). If it is not, Christianity becomes just another 'self improvement' religion.

Years ago, I joined a new, swanky gym thanks to a special offer. On my first visit, a personal trainer measured me up – chest, biceps etc. The reason? So, at the end of a specified programme, I could be measured again and see the muscles where once there were not even places! A 'before and after' approach, we might say. It did not quite happen as I hoped because, although there was nothing wrong with the 'before and after' idea, it was the 'in-between' that was the real problem. Moreover, I did notice a temptation, in the early days of training, subtly beginning to arise. I was undoubtedly becoming fitter, and it made me feel good some days and bad others. Though I hate to admit it, I was also feeling judgmental about others who did not seem to worry that they looked so out of shape. Eventually, when I began to realise what I would really need to do to have a body like an Adonis, I decided to await the resurrection instead! Spiritually, here's legalism. You begin to push *yourself*, to measure *yourself* up, to compare *yourself* to others. When we do that physically in a gym, there's a constant oscillation between pride (I'm better than him!) or despair (I'll never be as good as her!) The reason has been italicised – *yourself*, the 'Great Ego' centre-page, not Christ, the 'Great I am' centre-stage.

Hard as it is to admit it, there are 'grace killers' around in many churches today, evangelical ones included. If challenged theologically, such evangelical 'grace killers' will probably give the correct answers about the death of Jesus being sufficient. But legalism has many disguises when it invades Christian experience. It sets out its boundary markers of what it deems important. Take dress codes, for instance. A man approached me after I had preached in the church I pastored in East London, many years ago now. 'Pastor, if I may say so', his American accent helping me to locate his background, 'dressed like that, you wouldn't have been allowed to preach in my church.' I was a little taken aback, as I'm generally a suit, collar and tie merchant when conducting Sunday services. 'You see', he continued, 'you're not wearing a vest!' I assured him I was. 'No, not a 'T' shirt. I mean a waistcoat! Oh, and by the way your hair is too long as well!' I'm just glad I wasn't the pastor of his church. Legalism has many guises and disguises, 'vests' included! So how do we combat it?

● *In what ways might legalism appeal to a) someone who attends church infrequently and knows there are elements in their lifestyle that are not in line with the Scriptures (e.g. sleeping with a partner); b) the elder who is trying to keep their church afloat after the pastor's infidelity and subsequent resignation?*

STANDING FIRM

'Freedom' and 'slavery' are two terms we met repeatedly in 4:21-31. Verse 1 here is the link back to that and forward to more cautionary words. By a 'yoke of slavery' Paul means 'the whole law' (v3). So is Paul, to use a technical phrase, 'antinomian', that is 'against the law', the law which he knew God had given by revelation to Israel, 'inscribed by the finger of God' (Ex. 31:18)? No and Yes. No, because the law itself is 'holy, righteous and good' (Rom. 7:12) so far as it goes. The law is like buying a book on keeping fit. You can read the book, but that doesn't make you fit. You may study it line by line, perhaps discovering that it was originally written in German, which you proceed to learn to understand it better. The book outlines all the benefits of keeping fit but, in itself, cannot deliver what it sets out. Imagine, however, that it promised that one day a personal trainer would arrive who would take you by the hand and become your Mr Motivator to deliver what the training manual promised. The law, we recall, 'was put in charge to lead us to Christ' that we might be 'justified by faith' (3:24). But herein lay the Galatians' temptation. Instead of relying on Christ, they were 'trying to be justified' by law and risked losing Christ as a result (v4). So was Paul 'against the law'? The answer is 'Yes', if the law is viewed as the way to being right with God. So, which shall we choose, the 'yoke of slavery' or Christ's yoke that ' is easy and . . . light' (Mt. 11:28-30)?

DON'T RELAPSE

Paul is not speaking about a minor surgical procedure undertaken for medical reasons when he mentions circumcision (vs 2,3). Rather, it is the religious significance of such a rite willingly entered into: circumcision is a badge of obligation 'to obey the whole law' (v3). Why would anyone willingly sign up to that? The answer is a technique used by any form of proselytisation, political or religious. It is called 'gradualism.' Within the Galatian context, gradualism may have expressed itself something like this. Step one: 'If you want to be a real Christian, you ought not to eat pork. See if you don't feel better without it.' Step two: 'You know you ought to observe the Sabbath: no long journeys for you on the Sabbath, remember?' Step three: 'This is a big ask, and painful, but you know it makes sense. After all, forget that baptism stuff: it is circumcision that really counts.' And so on and on and on.

Paul will have none of this gradualism: 'neither circumcision nor uncircumcision has any value' (v6). Why? Because 'DIY' religion cannot deliver. It makes Christ 'of no value to you at all' (v2), alienating people from Jesus, so they are 'fallen away from grace' (v4). In contrast, 'by faith we eagerly await through the Spirit the righteousness for which we hope' (v5), which ultimately entails 'eternal life' (6:8) and 'a new creation' (6:15). Does that mean, in the meanwhile, that we just became lazy, good-for-nothing Christians as a result? How can that be when true faith that rests on Christ is a busy, living, active motivational force, 'expressing itself through love' (v6)?

'Fallen away from grace' (v4) is a strong warning to these would-be legalists. Did Paul believe that true believers could be 'saved and lost', or was he into 'once saved, always saved'? One's answer will be determined by a whole network of biblical and theological considerations, way outside the remit of this modest book. In context, however, the phrase may mean something like this. 'Given your present mindset, you are thinking and behaving as if Christ had not died (2:21), the Spirit had not been given (3:2) and you were still slaves (4:7). As a result, your present experience of seeking to live an authentic Christian life is disastrous.'

If we link the foregoing interpretation to the picture of 'running a race' and being 'cut in on' (v7), then we can see that legalism distracts us from 'obeying the truth' of the gospel in personal experience (v7). By its very nature, legalism is energy-sapping, for it does not enable us to 'throw off everything that hinders' and concentrate on 'the race marked out for us.' Rather than fixing 'our eyes on Jesus' (Heb. 12:1,2), finding his resources for the race, it makes us focus on ourselves and other resources outside of Christ. But such 'persuasion' to deviate from Christ does not 'come from the one who calls you' (v8), God himself. By its very nature, false teaching is pervasive, like yeast (v9) which (with one or two possible exceptions such as Matthew 13:33) always has a negative connotation in the Bible (Mk. 8:15, 1 Cor. 5:6,7).

Paul could never be accused of 'pulling his punches' when faced with major error. Heresy was and is as pernicious as leaven and its perpetrators 'will pay the penalty' whoever they were (v10). It is possible to tone down Paul's statement in verse 12 to read something like, 'I wish they would cut themselves off from you.' Bravely, however, the NIV's 'go the whole way and emasculate themselves' is almost certainly what Paul had in mind. The priests of the goddess Cybele were found in different parts of the Empire, Galatia included. They were, by dint of their office, all emasculated. It's as if Paul is saying that the Judaisers' legalism was no better than paganism (4:3,9).

If his words strike us today as intolerant, politically incorrect and in need of a 'makeover', such a reaction probably says more about ourselves and our time where anything goes. Paul believed in 'truth' (v7) and was a 'Mr Valiant-For-Truth', the character in Bunyan's famous work, *Pilgrim's Progress*, who declared 'I have fought his battles who will now be my rewarder.' This is not a plea for ungraciousness and insensitivity. Paul is still addressing 'brothers' (v11) and remains confident that they will come to see things clearly once again (v10). But how can that happen if error is not confronted and exposed for what it is, 'a different gospel' (1:6)? Before anyone writes Paul off as 'unchristian', study carefully the Master's own spiritual body-scan of his contemporaries' religious attitudes – Matthew 23.

● *Read Matthew 23 and consider what we can learn from*
 Jesus' non-compromising stance?

STAY FOCUSED

We should not underestimate the personal cost to Paul for faithfulness to the truth. The phrase 'still preaching circumcision' (v11) possibly refers to Paul's pre-Christian days. Or, more embarrassingly for him, according to his opponents, it may be a reference to his circumcision of Timothy (Acts 16:3), although whether that incident preceded this letter is unlikely. What is clear is the fact that Paul's unwillingness to be found 'still preaching circumcision' had its own pay-back system: he was 'still being persecuted' (v11). Why? In essence, circumcision was a short-hand statement for human effort and religion, as we have seen. Without Christ, any religious ritual can become a source of pride and self-flattery. At rock bottom, few of us believe we really are as bad or helpless as the Bible portrays. We often believe we are just as good as the next, and a whole lot better than many, and could be as good as the few if only we wanted to be. Then the gospel comes along and says things that knock us off our perch. It is summarised by the phrase 'the offence of the cross' (v11), literally its 'scandal.' That which 'scandalises' us, that highlights so well our human self-sufficiency, is the assertion that the only way for humanity to be rescued and stay rescued is to be totally dependent on God himself. This God of 'grace' (v4) has gone to extraordinary lengths. He has come into our world in his Son (4:4) and, as the long-awaited Messiah, he became 'a curse for us . . . hung on a tree' so we could be 'redeemed' (3:13). A murdered Messiah was a 'stumbling block' (literally 'scandal') to Jews and 'foolishness to Gentiles' but to all who believe, Jesus Christ is still 'the power of God' for salvation (1 Cor. 1:23,24).

Paul remains confident about their recovery (v10) as he holds the cross before them because, in Isaac Watt's words, it enables us 'to pour contempt on all my pride.' That's the very thing that 'circumcision' and any 'save yourself' religion never does. Some time ago, I was chatting to a minister who hails from North Wales, and discovered he was a fellow Evertonian. He asked me whether I knew the church near Goodison Park, Everton's ground, with 'the great big cross outside.' I did. He went on to tell me that when he regularly attended games in the sixties, he had an arrangement for meeting up with his pals if they were separated. 'If we get lost in the crowd, I'll meet you under that big cross.' When we are lost in the crowd of human sinfulness, failure and pride, God stands ready to meet us at 'the great big cross' of Jesus.

CONCLUSION

We return to Elsa the lioness as we conclude this section. The first time I saw her in *Born Free*, the film ended with her release back into the wild along with her cubs. But in real life she was literally a caged lion, born free but living in captivity. It is possible for legalism to do that to us, our family and our church. The antidote is to 'plant your feet firmly within the freedom Christ has won for us, and do not let yourself be caught again in the shackles of slavery' (v1, JBP).

FURTHER STUDY
Read Luke 4:18,19 and John 8:32,36. Do you feel as if in any area of your life you are restricted, oppressed or struggling to see the way forward? Trust in Jesus. He has come to set us free.

REFLECTION AND RESPONSE
- 'Pride goes before a fall', goes the saying, echoing Proverbs 16:18. The antidote? 'Humble yourselves under God's mighty hand' (1 Pet. 5:6). Otherwise? Remember today's proud peacocks may be tomorrow's feather dusters. Who'd want to be a duster when God is willing to clean us up?

- Jesus said his yoke was easy and his burden was light. He came to give us rest (Mt. 11:28,29). Do you ever feel as if you are labouring under a yoke that perhaps Jesus has not asked you to shoulder? Bring it to Jesus now.

- How can we maintain the freedom we have found in Christ? Seek the presence of God and walk in the way of his peace, keeping in step with his Spirit. Remember, you are showing your faith by expressing it through love, not by obligation.

SMALL GROUP DISCUSSION POINT
How free are you encouraged to be within your church? Be honest. If someone asks you to do something in your fellowship, and you don't feel it is something God wants you to do, do you feel like a bad Christian when you say no? How far are we still trusting in works, perhaps to gain the approval not of God, but of our fellow Christians?

CHAPTER 16

Striding Edge Christianity

GALATIANS 5:13-25

Aim: To encourage us to live in step with the Spirit

FOCUS ON THE THEME:
I was in the Lake District on an Outward Bound course, and our party was upward bound on Helvellyn, the 3118 foot high peak five or so miles east of Keswick. We were to approach the summit via Striding Edge, a ridge with hundreds of feet dropping away on either side. It was an icy, misty day and in places the path became precariously narrow. If I recall the details correctly, about half way along is a memorial plaque to a man who fell from the ridge and fatally descended to the valley below. Do you know from which side of Striding Edge he fell? In truth, it doesn't matter. If you fall from either side, the result is the same – almost certain death.

Do you think it is possible for someone who knows Jesus and is living for him to want to sin?

Reading: Galatians 5:13-26
Key verse: Galatians 5:25

So far in this letter, Paul has particularly opposed those who wanted to tempt these Galatians into a life under law, legalism. Paul's antidote has been the gospel of God's grace. But grace is dangerous. It might leave us with the impression that our behaviour does not matter. Rasputin, variously described as the 'holy man of Russia' and 'the mad monk', believed 'It is a privilege to do whatever your evil heart wants to do . . . It is right to serve sin.' In reacting against legalism, it is possible to go to the other extreme and fall into licence. Elsewhere, Paul asks, 'Shall we go on sinning, so that grace may increase?' (Rom. 6:1). Some in Galatia were tempted to answer 'Yes!' Paul, in this section, will show that such a course is as disastrous as legalism. But if we 'keep in step with the Spirit' (v25), we will stay on the Striding Edge of Christian freedom. We will avoid falling either side into the dark valleys below of legalism or licence. How? Step carefully this way!

A LICENCE TO KILL?

Freedom is dangerous! It can be abused so we 'indulge the sinful nature' (v13), a phrase used a number of times (vs 16,17,19,24). 'Sinful nature' is what everyone born into this world possesses. It affects every part of our being – physically, emotionally, mentally and spiritually. Not 'to indulge the sinful nature' (v13) means I do not allow it to strengthen its base in my life, very much like an army might to launch its offensives. When it comes to maintaining Christian freedom, this is total war, since the life of the Spirit is 'contrary to' and 'in conflict with' this sinful nature (v17). It's important to digest the practical implications for Christian identity and living. When we become followers of Jesus, we no longer need to 'gratify the desires of the sinful nature' (v16), since we have a new nature. Now 'we live by the Spirit' (v25). But the old nature has not been removed from us, that's why there still is conflict (v17).

Clearly, some in Galatia had grasped the revolutionary implications of the gospel for personal freedom. Their mistake was to presume such freedom had no boundaries: they could do whatever they pleased. The results were shocking. They were 'biting and devouring each other'– strong and graphic words (v15). According to a recent report, giant sheat fish, which can measure up to two metres in length (nearly seven feet) and weigh in at three hundred kilos (660 lbs), have been playing havoc with other wildlife in and around the Po River in Italy. They devour carp, eels, ducks, rats, kittens – anything they can get their teeth into. They have been known to charge at anglers and their boats. And guess what? There are times when they attack and eat each other!

A local church is meant to be a foretaste of heaven on earth. However, when freedom is used to indulge the sinful nature, a church can resemble a battlefield where we are firing at each other and shooting our own wounded. That's what some were doing in Galatia nearly two thousand years ago – and you thought they were the 'good old days'? Freedom is not a 'licence to kill', to have my own way no matter who gets hurt. What had gone wrong? These Christians simply underestimated the continuing power and effects of their sinful nature. Like the fictional '007', James Bond, they thought they had a 'licence to kill' and could therefore be a law unto themselves.

● *Read Romans 7:14-25. How does it encourage you to know that even the apostle Paul struggled with his old nature?*

A LAW UNTO THEMSELVES

In one of his homilies (sermons), St Augustine of Hippo said, 'Love and do what you like.' He meant that if we love God and our 'neighbour' as ourselves (v14), then we would find we have new likes. Unfortunately, some of these believers had only got the second half – 'do what you like.' Although legalism is prevalent in many churches today, other churches, in reaction to a moribund Christianity, have become so laid-back and casual that they are indistinguishable from the culture around them. Whether in 'legalist' or 'laid back' churches, sadly immorality, indiscipline and church splits are all too common. Helpfully, verses 19-21 run an ECG over the human heart and provide a Christian health check. The list given, seventeen in the KJV, fifteen in the NIV/RSV, is not exhaustive but illustrative – 'and the like' (v21). So, what does a life without the Spirit look like? At first glance, the words suggest immense vitality, action and energy. Here are people who are 'living it up', the lifestyle portrayed being 'obvious' (v19). Its consequences, however, are ultimately deadly (v21).

'The acts of the sinful nature' (v19) is a plural, and seems to be in deliberate contrast to the 'fruit of the Spirit' (v22), 'fruit' being in the singular. Life that is dominated by the sinful nature/flesh is a life that is made up of many bits that do not fit together. It becomes ragged, unintegrated and can easily fall apart. In contrast, to be under the Spirit of God's control is to experience a life that by grace is being integrated, putting us back together again, gluing us to Christ and each other. When my son, Paul, was quite young he had a 'Mister Men' jigsaw game. There were four different 'Mister Men' and each had six detachable parts to him – head, body, arms and legs. The purpose of the puzzle was to ensure the child learned to put the right parts together so they ended up with an integrated 'Mister Man.' Cleverly, although each set of arms, legs etc looked similar, they were not interchangeable. Unless, that is, you were determined! You could force parts together that created a 'Mister Man Frankenstein', that looked like the result of spare part surgery. Likewise, life without God is ultimately anything but integrated. The parts do not quite fit and so wholeness cannot be achieved. Such 'misfits' cannot 'inherit the kingdom of God' (v21).

As we look at these 'acts' in a little more detail, it may be helpful to divide the catalogue into four categories: sexual, religious, inter-personal and social sins, though undoubtedly they overlap.

Sexual sins

Turning to the first category, 'sexual immorality' covers a multitude of sexual sins. It's an omnibus, catch-all phrase, whilst 'impurity' is more to do with the mind and imagination (Mt. 5:28) that may express itself in today's world in addiction to internet pornography and the like. 'Debauchery', however, is a type of behaviour where there is no shame. The person preaches what they practise, being totally blasé about their promiscuity. The ancient world was awash with sexual debauchery on an unimaginable scale. So early Christians were warned: 'But among you there must not be even a hint of sexual immorality' (Eph. 5:3). Did they take any notice? It is just a sheer fact of history that no movement has more revolutionised and raised the sexual standards of its day than the Early Church. A local church must be the safest and purest place on earth for children and adults. Is yours?

Religious sins

'Idolatry and witchcraft' are religious in nature, but were often directly linked to sexual promiscuity. Bowing down to 'graven images' is everywhere forbidden in Scripture – just read the incredibly withering assessment of idolatry in Isaiah 44:9-20. Idolatry not only covers bowing down to objects made of wood or metal. Since it includes anything that takes the place of God, many who have never bowed down to a *metal* idol have unwittingly bowed to a *mental* one: secular humanism, atheistic evolution, Marxism, capitalism, hedonism etc. Then there's 'witchcraft', translating a word that gives us our English 'pharmacology' – not that the two are directly related today! This covers 'the black arts', clairvoyancy, astrology, necromancy, superstitions and the like. Over the last thirty or so years, there has been an explosion of alternative spiritualities in the western world. But many of them would be categorised by what Paul terms 'the acts of the sinful nature.' Intriguingly, he does not call them 'works of the devil', perhaps because the emphasis here is on human responsibility and manipulation. Despite all our twenty-first century sophistication, people remain incurably religious, whether the devil turns up or not. For many people, some alternative spirituality has led them far away from God.

Interpersonal sins

Paul proceeds to eight examples of inter-personal breakdown. Let's think about just two of them; 'fits of rage' and 'selfish ambition.' What a world of pain is covered here. Temper tantrums have often led to violence in a public house or a private home. On the other hand, 'selfish ambition' may drive a man to the top of his career to the detriment of his work colleagues and the loss of his wife and family, because he is blinded by ambition that has no other motivation than raw self. Peruse this list: it contains some fairly respectable sins. Many churches would discipline a man for a 'one-night stand' but leave another's 'fits of rage' unchallenged. A woman may be excommunicated for a pregnancy outside of marriage, whilst a respectable lady's acid tongue, year after year, corrodes the fellowship.

Social sins

Finally, we come to 'drunkenness' – binge drinking, and 'getting wasted' would be the contemporary applications. It is closely linked to 'orgies.' Why? Since alcohol is a depressant, it diminishes our judgment because of its effects on the brain. How many people have woken up after a bottle party in a stranger's bed, innocence stolen, fidelity lost and an STD or pregnancy to recall the night they cannot remember?

Is Paul saying that Christians are incapable of such sins? Does a slip of the tongue or of one's sexual standards mean one is doomed? The answer is that it is 'those who live like this.' 'Live' means continue to do, practise, behave like this. It is the whole direction of a person's life, their lifestyle. Such may 'claim to know God, but by their actions they deny him' (Titus 1:16). So, how are we to live? Welcome to the kingdom of God.

● *How can we keep our minds pure, when so much around us is saturated with immorality, bearing in mind Jesus' teaching that uncleanness comes from the heart anyway?*

A NEW ADMINISTRATION

'The kingdom of God' (v21) is the most revolutionary concept in history. It reminds us that every other kingdom is provisional and doomed to obsolescence (Rev. 11:15). When we enter that kingdom through new birth (Jn. 3:3-7), simultaneously we are rescued from the 'dominion of darkness' and brought into 'the kingdom of light' (Col.1:12,13). Quite literally, 'we live by the Spirit' (v25) so that Christ may be 'formed' in us (4:19). We are now under new ownership, being 'led by the Spirit' (v18). What we now need to learn is how to 'keep in step with the Spirit' (v25), for God's set purpose is to reproduce the life of Christ in us. What does that look like? It looks very much like 'the fruit of the Spirit' (v22).

We can usefully divide this ninefold fruit of the Spirit into three groups of three – the directly spiritual, the more social and the particularly selfward graces of Christlikeness.

The spiritual

First up is 'love', the virtue that teaches us to love because we have first been loved by God himself (1 Jn. 4:19). It is so *wide* that it knows no barriers of sex, social standing or race (3:28); so *deep* that no-one is so low and fallen that it cannot stoop to serve and lift such (Jn. 13:1-17); so *long* that it goes the distance from here to eternity; so *high* that there is no mountain it will not scale for Jesus.

Next, there's 'joy.' This is not mere good humour, the joy of life or camaraderie. Rather, it is an 'at homeness with God' that rises above the circumstances of pain and disappointment and produces 'songs in the night' (Job 35:10), even when one has been beaten severely and thrown in gaol (Acts 16:25ff). Richard Wurmbrand, author *Tortured for Christ*, was imprisoned and tortured over a period of fourteen years in Romanian communist gaols. Yet he testified how each night he would dance in his cell for joy in God, something that was totally independent of his circumstances and inexplicable, humanly speaking.

Then there's 'peace', a tranquility of heart and mind that is based on the gospel that gives 'peace *with* God' (Rom. 5:1) and grants 'the peace *of* God' (Phil. 4:6,7). In the storms of life, it hears Jesus say, 'Peace I leave with you; my peace I give you . . . Do not let your hearts be troubled' (Jn. 14:27).

Social graces

How necessary these are for relationships. Take 'patience', the quality that is 'slow to anger' like God himself (Ex. 34:6). Once upon a time we had a rather vicious cat. Dare to touch him and he growled like a dog and was likely to attack, claws and fangs at the ready! Some Christians are like that cat. Instead, we are called to exhibit 'kindness', that is a generosity towards others no matter who they are. It is easy to damn the whole of the Church because of the latest scandal that has risen in some local fellowship. But the truth is that Christianity has a brilliant track record for its humaneness and graciousness (another way to translate the word) in its treatment of all sorts of people – slaves, women, children, prisoners, the sick, the disabled, and even animals and their welfare – check out Proverbs 12:10.

Christian faith makes us 'useful', yet another nuance of this word. At the same time, the Spirit produces 'goodness' in us. It is possible to appear 'squeaky clean righteous' and do the basics well enough, yet to have lost all human warmth and winsomeness en route. But 'goodness' can never do the bare minimum, or fail to go the second mile. It brings a bounteousness and warmth to our living, so 'we fight and do not heed the wounds, we give and do not count the cost', all for Jesus' sake.

Selfward disciplines

'Faithfulness' is good, old-fashioned reliability. In the old Chinese sealed writing, the image that expressed faithfulness was that of a man standing next to a mouth. Faithfulness is a person keeping their promises, for whom their word is their bond, the type of person on whom you can rely. And just in case that reliability descends into officiousness, it is necessarily married to 'gentleness', sometimes rendered 'meekness' in some of the older translations.

'Meekness' in English sounds too near to 'weakness', as if the Spirit produces in us a wimpish characteristic. Rather, 'gentleness' is power under control. I recently inherited a car that is capable of doing 155 mph! It can burn many other cars off the road. But I never exercise all that power. If I did, I might literally burn others and myself. 'Gentleness' is quite prepared to give others space and time when it has the power to do otherwise.

The 'meek' character is the one who is exercising our final virtue, 'self-control.' The word is drawn from the field of athletics. Any athlete who is hoping to win his event has learned to say 'No' to what may be quite legitimate for others. Paul modelled this virtue himself – see 1 Corinthians 6:12 and 9:24-27. Sir Arthur Thomson, in one of his books on marine life, suggested that there are only two types of life in the sea – swimmers and drifters. The latter goes wherever the current takes him, the former where they want to go. The Christian may often feel like they are swimming against the tide in a sea awash with paganism. They are! But the Spirit-controlled person is swimming not drifting.

- *Read the words of Jesus in John 15:1-8. What must we do to be fruitful?*
- *How might faithfulness be evident in the way we speak about or treat other Christians.*

CONCLUSION

Here are two lifestyles, two ways to live. To live 'the sinful nature' life, all I have to do is act naturally! But to see the life of Christ reproduced in me demands two major ingredients – crucifixion and supernatural power. With reference to the former, Paul says, 'Those who belong to Christ Jesus have

crucified the sinful nature with its passions and desires'
(v24). Crucifixion was a pitiless, painful but decisive act.
Like radiotherapy on a cancer, it did the trick. It killed off the
problem. I need to be pitiless with my sins, however painful
it is to say 'No' to temptation. I need to recall that it was
those very sins that brought the Lord Jesus from a throne
to a cross to deal with them. This is not merely self-denial of
a few pleasures over Lent. This is more: 'I no longer live but
Christ lives in me' (2:20), Jesus being the centre of my life.
How is that possible?

Seven times in this section Paul has mentioned the Spirit
(vs 16,17,18,22,25). Because of him we live, by him we are
led and through him we are empowered to 'keep in step'
(v25), so that the life of Christ, 'the fruit of the Spirit', is
produced in us. The other day, my son produced a
memorable surprise birthday present for me – a helicopter
flight piloted by one of his friends. I saw more of the south
coast of England in 35 minutes than I had seen in ages. I
can testify that it is 'a lot less bovver in a hover'! I simply
said 'goodbye' to the ground, trusted myself to the pilot
and flew because of a power greater than myself. Does this
mean I simply 'let go and let God' do it all? Of course not!
Rather, it's similar to how a marriage works. If both parties
only contribute on a 50%/50% basis, the relationship will
probably fail. For marriage to be good, it needs to be
100%/100% from both partners. I am the one who is called
to present my body to God 'as a living sacrifice' (Rom. 12:1),
which echoes the idea of crucifixion here. And I need to do
that daily. Likewise, the Spirit is the one who alone can
produce the life of God in us, so we need to 'keep in step'
with his promptings to be like Christ.

A father was telling his young son what a Christian was
and how Christians behave. 'Son,' he said, 'Christians never
lie, steal or cheat. They are full of love and goodness, joy
and peace. They never lose their temper and are always

kind and forgiving.' As he carried on with his description, the little boy's eyes grew wider and wider. When his Dad finished, the boy exclaimed, 'That's fantastic, Dad. Have I ever seen a Christian?' The 'acts of the sinful nature are obvious' (v19). Let's pray that the fruit of the Spirit may be equally evident in us. The world desperately needs to see a Christian!

FURTHER STUDY
Look again at the nine-fold fruit of the Spirit. Take some time to look through the Gospels and see how the fruit of the Spirit was in evidence in Jesus in the way he treated all the different kinds of people who came to him for help . . . and to hinder him.

REFLECTION AND RESPONSE
- We become like those we spend time with. Ask yourself, who do you spend the most time with during the week? What might happen if you spent more time with Jesus?

- When you think about the fruit of the Spirit, and then take a good look at your own life, do you become discouraged or keen to 'try harder'? That is religion. As we spend more time in prayer and the word of God, getting to know God's voice, we will be able to follow the prompting of the Spirit of God more readily. Then we will surely become more like him.

- Those who are fruitful will be 'pruned.' Are you in a time of pruning now? Remember, it is your loving Father in heaven who is doing the pruning and you can trust in him. Be encouraged that those who are pruned will bear even more fruit (Jn. 15:2).

SMALL GROUP DISCUSSION POINT
How easy is it to think we can work up the fruit of the Spirit, and how hard is it to trust that God will accomplish the fruit in us? Praise God for the fruit you see in your own life and in the life of

others. If you have time, think about John 14:1-8 and thank God that, as in the natural world, pruning results in greater fruitfulness. Pray for anyone who is struggling during a time of personal pruning.

CHAPTER 17

Intensive care and invisible earnings

GALATIANS 5:26-6:10

Aim: To examine our attitude towards the family of God as we let the Spirit transform our way of living

FOCUS ON THE THEME:
Write down all the things you like most about your church – the worship? Teaching? Encouragement to use your God-given gifts? Reflect on what you have written. Have you included the love shown between members of Christ's body?

Reading: Galatians 5:26-6:10
Key verse: Galatians 6:8

I had only been a Christian for a few months, but the words of a senior work colleague, even now after forty years, still sting and challenge me: 'There's often more fellowship found in a pub than a church', he observed. If 'the world desperately needs to see a Christian', our conclusion in the previous section, it also needs to see groups of Christians who are meant to be the living embodiment of the Jesus lifestyle, and whose fellowship gives the lie to my friend's observation. Such groups we call the local church, 'the family of believers' (v10). When a church works properly, it is the best place on earth to be, 'God's temple' (1 Cor. 3:16). That is why we urgently need not merely bigger but better, not only happier but healthier local churches. Indeed, one of the major purposes of the gospel is to form such communities of believers into the body of Christ from the divided and disjointed mass of humanity (so 3:28 and see also Ephesians 2:11-22 and Colossians 3:11). So how is a local church to work? This section highlights a number of areas.

● *'There's often more fellowship found in a pub than a church.' Do you think this is true? Why might it be? What might people find in a pub that they don't find within the community of believers?*

SOMETHINGS AND NOTHINGS

God's purpose for his Church is to produce the life of Christ in believers, 'the fruit of the Spirit . . . by the Spirit' (5:22,25). Unfortunately, 'Murphy's Law' – if things can go wrong, they will go wrong – continues to operate because of the 'sinful nature' (5:17) which seeks to reassert itself in whatever ways it can. In this section, that nature manifests itself in conceit (v26), the antithesis of gentleness/humility (5:23). Spiritual pride is nothing new, like the man who wrote a book entitled *The world's seven greatest saints – and how I trained the other six!* Of course, such an attitude is a form of self deception (v3), and a million miles away from the One who said, 'I am gentle and humble in heart', though he was the very Son of God (Mt. 11:29). When pomposity gets hold of a church, Christians can quickly descend into 'provoking and envying each other' (v26). Indeed, the local church quickly does become indistinguishable from the local pub because a spirit other than the Spirit of God has taken control.

The Bible elsewhere warns against those who are 'wise in their own eyes and clever in their own sight' (Is. 5:21).

Some of these Galatians clearly were, hence the stinging rebuke, 'If anyone thinks he is something when he is nothing, he deceives himself' (v3). Behind that rebuke lies the whole background of the epistle. The cross, in which Paul boasted (6:14), is the death knell to human pride: we can do nothing to save ourselves. But the false teachers' 'persuasion' tactics (5:8) sought to turn these believers into religious robots who would feel good about themselves because they could do something – keep the law, signified by circumcision. The result, then and now, is always the same – pride kicks in. It parades itself as conceit (v26) because, in comparison 'to somebody else', I may appear better (v4). Or, more subtly, we can become smug about our 'humility.' In his brilliant *The Screwtape Letters*, C.S. Lewis introduces us to 'the patient', a Christian, who is feeling rather humble. Screwtape, the senior tempter, advises Wormwood, his assistant, to draw the patient's attention to such humility so he can then feel rightly proud of it! In contrast, the gospel teaches us that we are what we are by the grace of God (1 Cor. 15:10). So, what are we to do when somebody is 'caught in a sin' (v1)? Like 'Lucozade', we are to aid recovery.

● *What is true humility? Do those who show it know that they do so? Or do we have to forget about ourselves entirely in order to be truly humble?*

AIDING RECOVERY

It was Martin Luther who drew attention to the fact that the Christian is *simul iustus et peccator*, simultaneously right with God and still sinful. How right he was, for this side of heaven no-one is perfect. So, when a fellow believer stumbles, what is to be done? 'Brothers, if someone is caught in a sin, you who are spiritual should restore him gently. But watch yourself, or you also may be tempted' (v1). 'Caught in a sin' is helpfully paraphrased as doing 'something wrong . . . on a sudden impulse' (NEB). This is some kind of unspecified lapse that is inconsistent with life in the Spirit – financially, domestically, sexually etc. Such things happen, and when they do the spiritually mature are to deal with the situation in the first instance. Who are they? The kind of people who measure up to the qualities of leadership that 1 Timothy 3:1-13 outlines. And what precisely are they to do?

'Restore' is a rich word. In the NT it is used of mending nets, so they are 'fit for purpose' once more (Mk. 1:19). Outside the NT, the word had a medical meaning – setting right broken bones. The addition of 'gently' echoes 'gentleness' (5:23). This is not a ministry for those who are 'bulls in a china shop.' Rather, when someone has spiritually hit the wall, that person (and maybe their family too) need people who will 'not break' the 'bruised reed', the very ministry of the Lord Jesus (Is. 42:3; Mt. 12:20).

However, a spiritual recovery service is dangerous for the leaders involved: 'watch yourself, or you may also be tempted' (v2). There are at least two ways to understand this warning. The first is like a doctor who attends a highly infectious patient and catches the very disease they are seeking to cure. I have known of more than one pastor who, in seeking to deal with a member's marriage problems, has become involved in an affair. The alternative understanding is captured by Phillips's paraphrase: 'not with any feeling of superiority.' In other words, the leaders may begin to feel so good about themselves in comparison to this 'sinner' – a touch of the elder brother in the parable of the prodigal son (Lk. 15:29). 'So, if you think you are standing firm, be careful that you don't fall!' is a warning every Christian needs to take to heart (1 Cor. 10:12). A good local church is not a place where failure is never known but where it is biblically and spiritually dealt with. In that sense, it is like a hospital where you expect to find sick people who are recovering. Indeed, it is more akin to a 'field hospital' where casualties of war are being treated because of the 'conflict' we are in (5:17). Are there limits to that treatment? Yes, and they are found between two phrases, 'other's burdens' (v2) and 'his own load' (v5).

● *When helping others who are going through a time of trouble, how might you effectively protect yourself from self-righteous behaviour, pride, or getting caught up in the same sin yourself?*

BURDENS AND RESPONSIBILITY

The picture behind 'burden' (v2) is that of a huge load, the kind that an individual soldier, to retain the military metaphor of the last paragraph, is unable to carry. It is something overwhelming though unspecified. A major illness, a divorce, a financial crisis resulting from the loss of a job, bereavement etc, all spring to mind. At such times, the local church can be stunning in its intensive care for each other, 'to those who belong to the family of believers' (v10). By the time our daughter, Ruth, was born, my wife, Brenda, had already been diagnosed with multiple sclerosis. For the first six months of Ruth's life, Monday to Friday from 8 am to 2 pm, Elsie, an elder's wife, was at our home doing anything and everything she could so I could continue to operate as the pastor of that church. And it did not finish there, for Elsie or others in the fellowship: 'Let us not become weary in doing good' (v9). I lost count of the meals and babysitting etc we were on the receiving end of for the next few years in that great church in East London.

Moreover, there was nothing exclusive about such caring in that fellowship: 'Therefore, as we have opportunity, let us do good to all people' (v10). I witnessed 'good' being exercised towards so many in that cosmopolitan area of London, as the church reached out with the gospel of Christ and let its light shine via its good works to all sorts of people (Mt. 5:13-16). Are there are any limits imposed on such 'care in the community'? Yes, there are.

I can recall more than one occasion where people have been disappointed with the level of care they felt they have received in churches I have served. One couple demanded to know why no-one in the church was willing to look after their three children for free, whilst they both worked so they could send some of their money 'back home.' The answer was straightforward, 'each one should carry his own load' (v5). The individual soldier cannot be expected single-handedly to transport all the parts of a Bailey bridge. But he is expected to 'shoulder his own pack' (JBP), his own kit. Of course, there are times when he may be 'wounded' and cannot do even that, hence verse 1. But such is the exception to the general rule. Every Christian will have their individual responsibilities that cannot be devolved to the local church. It is all part of sowing and reaping.

● *There's a fine line to draw between carrying someone's burdens in a time of crisis and yet letting them carry their own load in day-to-day life. How can we be alert and sensitive to real need and yet encourage 'shouldering your own pack' within the church, especially when someone has a long-term need such as debt, loneliness, physical problems or emotional insecurity?*

KEEPING AN EYE ON THE HARVEST

Many people are myopic, short-sighted. They live in a world of the 'now', immediate gratification, if at all possible. In contrast, Christians are to be people who take the long-term view, 'we will reap a harvest if we do not give up' (v9). I suspect that I am one of the world's worst gardeners. My horticulture difficulties began when I was about six years of age in inner city Liverpool. My school teacher announced that each of us were to bring in bulbs for planting. I have a faint recollection of turning up with a forty-watt type. I lit up the class! However, even I learned three things early on: if you don't sow, you won't reap; what you do reap is determined by what you sow; and you do not sow and reap in a day, it takes time. We six-year olds had to wait for those mysteriously planted bulbs to reappear as beautiful flowers.

If it is true in the natural sphere that we have 'to speculate to accumulate', it holds good in the spiritual realm too. Take the thorny issue of what is called 'ministerial stipends' – 'Anyone who receives instruction in the word must share all good things with his instructor' (v6). The Lord Jesus reminds us that 'the worker deserves his wages' for gospel work (Lk. 10:7; 1 Cor. 9:14). A good general rule is that Christian workers dependent on a congregation should live around the economic level of those whom they serve. There are many parts of the world where leaders eke out a living 'on the bread line' with their congregations who are likewise poor. Generally speaking, that is not the situation in most of the western world. Here, I suspect, every Christian worker will have their store of financial horror stories. I recall a friend of mine from college days over thirty years ago lamenting the financial treatment of her Dad, a full-time Christian worker, and its knock-on effects to her family. 'We always seemed to have second-hand clothes, second-hand shoes, second-hand everything, while all the other kids in church had everything new.' I know churches which seem happy to keep their pastor on family credit and income support, not because the church is very small (that might be understandable) but because they believe, or so it seems, that the leader will be keener if they are hungry. Shameful! In contrast, such 'doing good' (v9) is not only part of a bigger picture to 'all people' and 'the family of believers' (v10), as we have noted, but also part of a vital principle, reaping 'a harvest' (v9). What determines that?

'Do not be deceived: God cannot be mocked. A man reaps what he sows' (v7). Isn't God mocked every day? Rather, in this context, it means, 'No one makes a fool of God' (The Message). But doesn't 'grace' negate the 'law' of sowing and reaping? Yes and no. Yes, when we are justified, we are acquitted (re-read especially 3:10-14). No, for 'the law of Christ' (v2), which is 'faith expressing itself in love' for my 'neighbour' (5:6,14) has its own rewards or otherwise: 'The one who sows to please his sinful nature, from that nature will reap destruction; the one who sows to please the Spirit, from the Spirit will reap eternal life' (v8). Although other interpretations are possible, I think that what we are being reminded of and challenged about here is the whole area of our individual stewardship – our time, talents and treasure. How do we 'sow' them, to the 'sinful nature' or 'to please the Spirit'? What are our long term investments in, items that will be invisible earnings for the kingdom or in stuff that we cannot take with us?

Sir John Laing was a well-known, wealthy and respected Christian businessman. Early in his business career, he set himself a 'programme for my life', as he put it, and which he summarised: 'First the centre of my life was to be God – God as seen in Jesus Christ. Secondly, I was going to enjoy life, and help others to enjoy it.' After he died in January

1978, this multi-millionaire's published will detailed his net estate at £371. All around the world today, there are countless Christian churches, organisations and individual believers, myself included, who have benefited from the stewardship of a man who sought to 'please the Spirit.'

- *Life is not easy for some people, financially, emotionally etc. Think of some known to you. How can you help those who are struggling, to sow today so they might reap a better tomorrow?*

- *Think about how you can sow to please the Spirit in your life, and write down anything that comes to mind. Can you implement any of your ideas today, this week, this month, this year?*

Liverpool Football Club (this is a painful illustration for an Evertonian!) has a marvellous programme they run called 'Truth4Youth.' It has some wonderfully catchy titles for articles dealing with issues facing young people: 'Give racism the red card'; 'Before you please, think disease' etc. One is particularly appropriate for any group of Christians (besides 'You'll never walk alone'!) – 'We is better than me.' The article talks about an acronym that the Club uses, T.E.A.M.– Together Each Achieves More. This is precisely the kind of teamwork the Lord requires of every local church, so that together they intensively care and invisibly earn for the kingdom in their community.

- *There are a number of 'Lone Ranger' Christians who have become isolated for many different reasons. Do you know any? What first steps might you consider in inviting them back into the team?*

FURTHER STUDY

Read and think about Job 4:8, Proverbs 11:18 and 22:8, Hosea 10:12, and 2 Corinthians 9:6. What are you sowing into your life in the area of relationships or attitudes that might affect your Christian witness today – and also in the future?

REFLECTION AND RESPONSE

- Do you have the opportunity today to do good to a) all people and b) the family of believers?

- In what ways can we begin to sow today to please the Spirit so we might reap a good harvest later, both personally, for our family, our church, and for the kingdom of God? Ask God what he wants to sow into your life today and trust his Spirit to bring that about in you as you keep in step with and obey him.

- Buy a packet of seeds you can grow on your windowsill (such as parsley, basil or cress). As you watch them grow, be reminded that we reap what we sow personally, practically and spiritually.

SMALL GROUP DISCUSSION POINT

Spend some time in prayer asking God that your church might become a truly healthy place where the injured and wounded by life might find acceptance, rest and restoration. What is your fellowship sowing that it might reap in years to come? Finish by organising something you can do as a team, whether this is getting involved in evangelism/further prayer, or just going for a meal/going bowling and enjoying time together.

CHAPTER 18

The marks of the crucified

GALATIANS 6:11-18

Aim: To remember that what counts in our Christian lives is the new creation

---

FOCUS ON THE THEME:
The Christian life is not about what we do, it is 'what *God* is doing, and he is creating something totally new, a free life!' (Gal. 6:15, The Message) Say this out loud several times. As you prepare for the last session in this study, let the truth of this statement wash over you. Go round the group asking them to finish the sentence 'I'm a Christian because. . .' The person who uses the least words is the winner.

Reading: Galatians 6:11-18
Key verse: Galatians 6:15

In George Orwell's classic *1984*, Winston Smith lives in London which is part of Oceania, one of the three countries into which the world is divided. It is a totalitarian state led by Big Brother and it controls and censors its citizens' behaviour, their thoughts included. Everywhere he goes, Smith is reminded 'BIG BROTHER IS WATCHING YOU.' Religion has its counterparts to this frightening Orwellian world, as any cursory glance at history will confirm. In Galatia, its form was the extreme righteousness of those we have called the Judaisers who sought to control the thoughts and behaviour of those whom Christ had set free (5:1). As Paul concludes his letter, he does not know whether its contents will 'do the trick', though he has expressed confidence that it would (5:10). Just in case, however, the epistle finishes with a bang not a whimper: 'See what large letters I use as I write to you with my own hand' (v11), a sentence that has been variously interpreted.

Hitherto, Paul has almost certainly been dictating his words to a scribe. Now he takes the quill himself to add something in his own hand, like we might do having typed a letter and wishing to personalise it or emphasise something. The 'large letters' may confirm Paul's eyesight was poor (4:13-15 and comments) or underline the immaturity of these converts, 'foolish Galatians' (3:1), who needed to be written to as if they were still in primary school. He is determined that they get the message because others are equally determined these Galatians should get theirs.

THE 'SPIN DOCTORS'

'Spin doctors' is a recent phrase used in English to describe those who can glaze the truth and put the appropriate twist on whatever needs to be communicated. They know how to bury the bad news in the good. Their predecessors, however, have been around a long time, Galatia in the first century included. Such people made 'a good impression outwardly', they had the appropriate sales pitch, in order to compel the Galatians 'to be circumcised' (v12). In itself, there is nothing wrong with good publicity and public relations, of course. Many church buildings (and people) would benefit from a makeover. But the real danger in Galatia was that the externals – all that the shorthand 'circumcision' represented – would replace Christ. Some churches give the impression that the decorum of their liturgy, the correct vestments being worn for the celebration of the Eucharist and services finishing on time are more important than their individual members becoming 'a new creation' (v15).

Inevitably, these Judaisers had a motive for their agenda: 'to avoid being persecuted for the cross of Christ' (v12). Like today in different parts of the world, the Jews in NT times were a respected minority community. They were recognised by the Roman Empire and had various dispensations to practise their religion officially. For instance, they did not have to bring an offering to a Roman shrine and proclaim 'Caesar is Lord.' Gentile Christians, unfortunately, had no such rights and dispensations. However, by undergoing circumcision, they would be able to demonstrate physically, if such need arose, that they were Jewish really, their faith being a sub-set of Judaism. When persecution threatened from whatever quarter, as the false teachers had discovered, circumcision was a potential 'get out of gaol free' card. They could shelter under the badge of circumcision, rather than in Christ and his cross. Unfortunately, experience reminds us, 'there's no such thing as the free lunch.' So, the 'get out of gaol free' cards were deceptive. They led to another prison, an obligation to 'obey the whole law' (5:3). Herein lay the irony of the Judaisers' offer: 'Not even those who are circumcised obey the law' (v13).

The Judaisers were offering an improved version of the basic Christian package, some higher or deeper life. Today, such offers usually have a strap line such as 'the key to . . .', 'the secret of . . . ' etc. Now as then, we need to beware of such inducements. If there were one 'key' or 'secret', why did God bother to give us a Bible with hundreds of keys and 'his very great and precious promises' (2 Pet.1:4)?

Sometimes, you will discover that the purveyor of that particular 'key to' has failed to take the treatment themselves, or has discovered that it didn't work anyway. If the Judaisers had their way, these Gentiles would soon be homogenised, all the same religious robots – always the mark of the cultic – trying to obey the law their new spiritual masters could not keep themselves. Unlike a one size fits all solution, the gospel offers me the Lord Jesus himself, in his entirety. There are times when I need his 'strokes', assuring me that all is well. Other times, I need his 'pokes', prodding me in the right direction. Sometimes I just need his 'folks', the people of God, some even with their 'jokes', to help me along the path of the 'law of Christ' (v2), that is, obedience and commitment to the gospel of grace.

Remarkably, there was yet another motivation beside self-preservation (v12) at work in these false teachers: 'they want you to be circumcised that they may boast about your flesh' (v13). Almost certainly, this points to some form of head count. In itself, there is nothing inherently wrong in collecting ecclesiastical statistics; try the book of Numbers or the church growth recorded in Acts (2:41, 4:4, 6:1 etc). In this case, however, there was something insidious, for it fuelled the boasting of these false teachers: 'look how many have come over to our understandings of things . . . Another five joined us last week, you know.' It was the Lord Jesus himself who drew attention to the missionary zeal of the Pharisees travelling 'over land and sea to win a single convert' and its consequential disastrous results for the new proselyte (Mt. 23:15). Our challenge is to ensure that we do not count people but realise that it is people who really count. As one man asked his Christian friend, 'Do you love me because you want me converted, or do you want me converted because you love me?' Paul could love people because of the One who had loved him (2:20) and revolutionised his life through the cross.

- *How do we know when it is the right time to invite people to Alpha courses or to a meeting at our churches? If they say No, what do we do then? How do we avoid having an attitude of scalp-hunting?*
- *Think about someone you like very much who is not a Christian. If they never became a Christian, would you still be their friend?*

THE 'WONDROUS CROSS'

In stark contrast to the Judaisers' boasting about 'flesh' (v13), Paul will never 'boast except in the cross of our Lord Jesus Christ' (v14). Separated by two thousand years from this statement about the cross, we can so easily sentimentalise Paul's words. In contrast, 'cross' and 'crucifixion' were anything but sentimental in the Roman world. It was a gruesome, ruthless form of death, invented by the Phoenicians and adopted by the Romans. It was the first century equivalent of the gallows, the electric chair, the burning at the stake, reserved for the worst offenders. Mel Gibson's film, *The Passion of the Christ*, has sought to bring some of its excruciatingly gruesome horrors to twenty-first century audiences. Why boast in that? Because this cross belonged to 'our Lord Jesus Christ' (v14). That cross acts like a mirror, for it reflects our true condition before a holy God. But through the cross, our debt has been paid, our sin has been atoned for, our curse has been removed and our death sentence has been met by Another (3:13, for instance). All this is objective – God has accomplished this for us in Christ. But the cross has a necessary subjective element for Paul, for through it, 'the world has been crucified to me, and I to the world' (v14).

The problem with the spin doctors of the previous verses is a temptation we all face: 'What do people think of me?'

So we are tempted to suppress our Christian witness. In addition, the attractiveness of the world remains. As John Ernest Bode confessed: 'I see the sights that dazzle, the tempting sounds I hear' (from, *O Jesus, I have promised*). But the revolutionary implications of the cross of Jesus had so invaded Paul's heart and mind that the opinions and applause of the world no longer determined his life. For him, the cross had become music to his soul. In Greek mythology, the Sirens were creatures whose irresistible song lured mariners to their destruction on the rocks around their island. The Argonauts escaped such doom because Orpheus, realising their peril, took his lyre and sang so beautifully that his song drowned out the fatal music of those Siren voices. Likewise, the cross of Jesus needs daily to be music to our ears: ensure you take time to tune in and listen.

Why is Paul so insistent about this? For the simple reason that only the cross of Christ delivers in terms of salvation: 'Neither circumcision nor uncircumcision means anything; what counts is a new creation' (v15). It is only through the death and resurrection of Jesus that people become 'a new creation.' Circumcision, religion, law or whatever cannot deliver that. It is the Living Christ alone who can apply all the benefits of his redemption by the Spirit to human hearts and lives. Elsewhere, Paul will draw attention to the objective, cosmic consequences of the cross through which the very universe will be renewed (Col. 1:15-20). Such renewal has already started in those who cry 'Abba, Father' (4:6). On such people 'who follow this rule', Paul wishes 'peace and mercy' (v16).

● *What do people think of Christians? Brainstorm a few ideas. How many of these criticisms have a kernel of truth in them, perhaps something we could address? How many should we ignore?*

'HAST THOU NO SCAR?'

'Grace' (v18), 'peace and mercy' (v16) are reserved for those who don't follow the rules but 'this rule', literally 'canon.' Originally, as we saw earlier, this was a standard used by a carpenter or surveyor to assess various measurements. The word is used now when we speak about 'the canon of Scripture', the books we acknowledge as the very words of God. That is a helpful use, for ultimately the question about any religious experience or truth claim, from whatever source, is whether such conforms to 'this rule', the gospel of Christ as faithfully recorded in the Bible. It is this gospel alone that grants me peace with my Maker, mercy for my sin and grace to live for Christ day by day. Paul adds, 'even to the Israel of God' (v16).

It would be possible to translate this last phrase as 'and to the Israel of God', so that Paul has in mind the physical Israel of his day, a prayer certainly worth praying. Other NT uses suggest that he is viewing all who believe in Messiah Jesus as the 'new' Israel of God (Eph. 2:14-22; Phil. 3:3). Whichever way one jumps in interpreting this phrase, controversy is bound to follow – anything but 'peace'! Recently, I have been helped by a book by Michael Eaton that sets out some of the issues. You may find it helpful too.[6]

Equally intriguing is Paul's reference to 'the marks of Jesus' (v17), literally 'the stigmata.' 'Stigmata' are the alleged physical wounds of Christ that various saints have exhibited over the centuries (there were some 321 recorded accounts up to the twentieth century). St Francis of Assisi, according to legend, was so overwhelmed in prayer by the love of Christ that his hands bore the nail marks of the Crucified afterwards and until his dying day. Similarly, a Hebrew Christian lady, whom I knew, exhibited something similar every Easter. That said, I am more persuaded that Paul had in mind the physical and emotional scars of his suffering for the gospel – check out 2 Corinthians 11:22-29, for instance. Whether they are physical, emotional or spiritual, few Christians escape scars if they consistently follow Christ. That great Irish missionary to India and poetess, Amy Carmichael, asks the question, 'Hast thou no scar?'

> Hast thou no scar?
> No hidden scar on foot, or side, or hand?
> I hear thee sung as mighty in the land,
> I hear them hail thy bright ascendant star,
> Hast thou no scar?
>
> Hast thou no wound?
> Yet I was wounded by the archers; spent,
> Leaned Me against a tree to die; and rent
> By ravening beasts that compassed Me, I swooned.
> Hast thou no wound?
>
> No wound? No scar?
> Yet, as the Master shall the servant be,
> And piercèd are the feet that follow Me.
> But thine are whole; can he have followed far
> Who hast no wound or scar?

How do we get to the place where we willingly follow the Lord Jesus come what may, scars included – all the bitternesses, disappointments and failures of life notwithstanding? For Paul and for us it is through delighting 'in the cross of our Lord Jesus Christ', and discovering 'the grace of our Lord Jesus Christ' being with our spirits (v18).

'GOODBYE GALATIANS, HELLO FREEDOM'

As we conclude this epistle, there are three questions we all need to answer personally: To whose authority do we submit? In which 'good news' do we believe? To what kingdom do we belong?

In the first couple of chapters, Paul has argued convincingly for his gospel, that it is not 'man made' but rather a 'revelation' from Jesus Christ (1:11,12). Many have challenged that assertion, both then and now. Is Christianity, as found in the pages of the NT, a gigantic fraud or a revealed religion? We will never follow Christ in the tough places of life unless we are convinced that the NT gospel is authoritative and reliable.

From the end of the second and into the next couple of chapters of Galatians, the primary focus was on the nature of the gospel and how we are justified before a holy God. Is it faith in Christ alone, or faith in my works alone or a combination of the two? Has Christ done enough, so I may sing, 'In Christ alone my hope is found'? If he has, then I am right with God. If he has not, then no-one else can possibly have done more and therefore we are a lost human race. Which gospel do we believe?

Finally, Paul's latter chapters show us how life in the Spirit is both possible and practical. Real Christian faith actually *works*, 'faith expressing itself through love' (5:6), so we 'serve one another in love' (5:13), seeking to 'do good to all people' (6:10). Instead of life being the fragmentary 'acts of the sinful nature' (5:19), as new creations (6:15), indwelt by the Spirit, his holistic 'fruit' is being produced in our lives (5:22,23). Such people 'inherit the kingdom of God' (5:21). Do we belong by God's grace to that kingdom?

'It is for freedom that Christ has set us free' this epistle thunders. In a world of slavery, economic, emotional and spiritual, in a world of hopelessness and despair where many fear Big Brother is Watching You, this letter reminds us that the Lord Jesus is Watching Over You, as Saviour, Liberator, Redeemer and Friend. *All you need is Christ* May that be your experience. Or, in the final word of the epistle, 'Amen' – so let it be!

● *Reflect on the three questions above: to whose authority do you submit? In which 'good news' do you believe? To what kingdom do you belong?*

FURTHER STUDY
Spend some time looking through the book of Galatians and remembering the points that really struck you during this study. It would be worth making notes (if you haven't already done so) while the study is fresh in your mind. How can you take what you have learned and really make it part of your daily Christian life?

REFLECTION AND RESPONSE
Remember that *we are accepted in God's family as co-heirs with Christ because of who Jesus is, not because of what we do.* Write that down somewhere and stick it on your desk, your dressing-table or your fridge. We cannot save ourselves or live to please him in our own power. He effected a rescue mission before we even realised we needed rescuing. Remember that grace is God's free, unmerited favour and praise him for his great love for you.

SMALL GROUP DISCUSSION POINT
Review together the things you have learned in this study. If your group decided to keep a journal at the start, look at it together. Ask each member of the group: What has been the most useful thing you have learned? What challenged you the most? How do you think what you have learned will help you sow to please the Spirit in your Christian life? Finish by praying the grace (2 Cor. 13:14).

1   J.B. Phillips translation
2   N.T. Wright, *Paul: Fresh perspectives* (London: SPCK, 2005)
3   P. Eveson, *The Great Exchange: Justification by faith alone in the light of recent thought* (Branby: Day One, 1996)
    M. Seifrid, *Christ our Righteousness: Paul's theology of justification* (Apollos, 2000)
4   Martin Luther King, Jr., *Strength to Love* (New York: Harper & Row, 1963), p34
5   Adrian Plass, *The Theatrical Tapes of Leonard Thynn* (London: Marshall, Morgan and Scott, 1989), pp20-21
6   Michael Eaton, *The Christian, Israel and the Hope of World Revival* (Tonbridge: Sovereign World, 2006)